PEOPLES
of
EASTERN ASIA

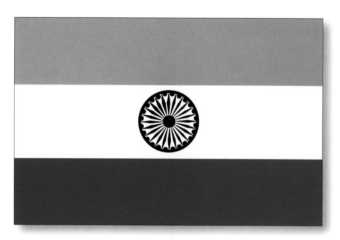

India

PEOPLES
of
EASTERN ASIA

Volume 4
India

MARSHALL CAVENDISH
NEW YORK • LONDON • SINGAPORE

Marshall Cavendish Corporation
99 White Plains Road
Tarrytown, New York 10591

www.marshallcavendish.com

©2005 Marshall Cavendish Corporation

Consultants:
    Emily K. Bloch, Department of South Asian Languages
        and Civilizations, University of Chicago
    Amy Rossabi, MA in Southeast Asian History
    Morris Rossabi, Professor and Senior Research Scholar,
        Columbia University

Contributing authors:
    Fiona Macdonald
    Gillian Stacey
    Philip Steele

Marshall Cavendish
    Editor: Marian Armstrong
    Editorial Director: Paul Bernabeo
    Production Manager: Michael Esposito

Discovery Books
    Managing Editor: Paul Humphrey
    Project Editor: Kate Taylor
    Design Concept: Ian Winton
    Designer: Barry Dwyer
    Cartographer: Stefan Chabluk
    Picture Researcher: Laura Durman

The publishers would like to thank the following for their permission to reproduce photographs:
    akg-images (British Library: 178; Jean-Louis Nou: 173, 174); Axiom (Francis Bacon: 200; Ian Cumming: 195; Sitting Images: 188); CORBIS 210 (Bettmann: 179, 183; Christie's Images: 181; Lindsay Hebberd: 220; Philadelphia Museum of Art: 176); Corbis Sygma (Baldev: 206; John Van Hasselt: 189); Hutchison (Carlos Freire: 219; Jeremy Horner: 196, 208, 211; Rajendra Shaw: 197); Panos (Jean-Leo Dugast: 201); Popperfoto: 184; David Simson – DASPHOTOGB@aol.com: 202, 203, 209, 212, 215, 222, 223; Still Pictures (Joerg Boethling: 171, 187, 218; N. Dunlop-Christian Aid: cover; Mark Edwards: 213, 214; John Isaac: 186, 207; Pant-UNEP: 194; Jorgen Schytte: 192; Rajendra Shaw-Christian Aid: 190); Trip (Dinodia: 182, 203, 204, 216, 217; B. Gibbs: 206; F. Good: 199; R. Graham: 172; H. Rogers: 177, 198, 205; B. Turner: 191, 215)

(cover) Cambodian Buddhist monks in Phnom Penh.

Editor's note: Many systems of dating have been used by different cultures throughout history. *Peoples of Eastern Asia* uses B.C.E. (Before Common Era) and C.E. (Common Era) instead of B.C. (Before Christ) and A.D. (Anno Domini, "In the Year of the Lord").

Library of Congress Cataloging-in-Publication Data

Peoples of Eastern Asia.
        p. cm.
    Includes bibliographical references and index.
    Contents: v. 1. Bangladesh-Brunei -- v. 2. Cambodia-China -- v. 3. China-East Timor -- v. 4. India -- v. 5. Indonesia -- v. 6. Japan-Korea, North -- v. 7. Korea, South-Malaysia -- v. 8. Mongolia-Nepal -- v. 9. Philippines-Sri Lanka -- v. 10. Taiwan-Vietnam.
    ISBN 0-7614-7547-8 (set : alk. paper) -- ISBN 0-7614-7548-6 (v. 1 : alk. paper) -- ISBN 0-7614-7549-4 (v. 2 : alk. paper) -- ISBN 0-7614-7550-8 (v. 3 : alk. paper) -- ISBN 0-7614-7551-6 (v. 4 : alk. paper) -- ISBN 0-7614-7552-4 (v. 5 : alk. paper) -- ISBN 0-7614-7553-2 (v. 6 : alk. paper) -- ISBN 0-7614-7554-0 (v. 7 : alk. paper) -- ISBN 0-7614-7555-9 (v. 8 : alk. paper) -- ISBN 0-7614-7556-7 (v. 9 : alk. paper) -- ISBN 0-7614-7557-5 (v. 10 : alk. paper) -- ISBN 0-7614-7558-3 (v. 11 : index vol. : alk. paper)
    1. East Asia. 2. Asia, Southeastern. 3. South Asia. 4. Ethnology--East Asia. 5. Ethnology--Asia, Southeastern. 6. Ethnology--South Asia.

DS511.P457 2004
950--dc22
                                                                                2003069645

    ISBN 0-7614-7547-8 (set : alk. paper)
    ISBN 0-7614-7551-6 (v. 4 : alk. paper)

Printed in China
09 08 07 06 05 04   6 5 4 3 2 1

Contents

INDIA

INDIA IS THE SEVENTH LARGEST COUNTRY IN THE WORLD.

The vast Himalayan mountain ranges stretch across northern India. Kanchenjunga is the third highest mountain in the world, at 28,169 feet (8,586 meters). Several of India's great rivers arise in the Himalayas: the Ganga, the Yamuna, and the Brahmaputra.

Just south of the Himalayas lie the flat river plains of northern India. The fertile soil of these plains is good for farming. Some of India's earliest civilizations developed here, and today it is the most heavily populated region of India.

In the northwest, between the Indus and the Ganga, lies a dry, barren land: the Great Indian, or Thar, Desert.

Southern India is known as peninsular India. At its heart lies the Deccan Plateau, a large upland area. On either side of the Deccan are mountain ranges: the Western and Eastern Ghats. Groups of tiny tropical islands also make up part of India: the Lakshadweep (luhk-SHAWD-weep) Islands in the Arabian Sea and the Andaman and Nicobar Islands in the Bay of Bengal.

Two boys playing in the monsoon rain, Karnataka State, southern India. Although monsoon rains can cause flooding, farmers depend on them to water their crops.

Ancient India

Archaeological evidence shows that humans first existed in India between approximately 400,000 B.C.E. and 200,000 B.C.E. At first they lived by gathering plants and berries and hunting wild animals. By about 4000 B.C.E some had begun to grow crops and domesticate animals and to settle in villages. At around this time, it seems that the first Dravidian (druh-VIH-dee-yuhn) peoples came from the west into the Indus (IHN-duhs) Valley region in the northwest of India.

The Indus Valley Civilization

The Dravidian peoples of the Indus Valley developed one of the world's first great civilizations—larger and possibly more advanced than ancient Egypt or Mesopotamia (meh-suh-poe-TAE-mee-uh). The Indus Valley civilization began about five thousand years ago, in the river valleys of northwest India (much of this area is

FACTS AND FIGURES

Official name: *Republic of India*

Status: *Independent state*

Capital: *New Delhi*

Major towns: *Ahmedabad, Bangalore, Mumbai, Kolkata, Hyderabad, Chennai*

Area: *1,269,345 square miles (3,287,604 square kilometers)*

Population: *1,029,991,000*

Population density: *811 per square mile (313 per square kilometer)*

Peoples: *72 percent Indo-Aryan; 25 percent Dravidian; 3 percent Mongoloid and other*

Official languages: *Hindi, English, and 14 other official regional languages (Assamese, Bengali, Gujarati, Kannada, Kashmiri, Malayalam, Marathi, Oriya, Punjabi, Sanskrit, Sindhi, Tamil, Telugu, and Urdu)*

Currency: *Rupee*

National days: *Republic Day (January 26); Independence Day (August 15)*

Country's name: India, *from the Indus River.*

Time line:	Nomadic peoples begin to settle in villages; first Dravidian peoples move into Indus Valley region in northwest India	Rise of great Indus Valley civilization, centered on cities of Mohenjo Daro and Harappa
	ca. 4000 B.C.E.	**ca. 3000–2500 B.C.E.**

CLIMATE

India lies between the Tropic of Cancer and the Equator. Most of the country has a tropical climate, and there are three main seasons: the hot season; the wet season; and the cool season. The climate can vary greatly, depending on the geography of the region. The north is generally cooler than the south, and around the Himalayas it often snows heavily during the cool season. Near India's coasts, the climate is wetter and more humid. Much less rain falls inland.

	Chennai	Mumbai (Bombay)	New Delhi	Kolkata (Calcutta)
Average January temperature:	77°F (25°C)	76°F (24°C)	57°F (14°C)	68°F (20°C)
Average July temperature:	87°F (31°C)	82°F (28°C)	88°F (31°C)	84°F (29°C)
Average annual precipitation:	50 in. (127 cm)	84 in. (213 cm)	29 in. (74 cm)	64 in. (163 cm)

now in Pakistan). At the heart of Indus culture were its cities, above all Mohenjo Daro (moe-HAEN-joe DAH-roe) and Harappa (huh-RAH-puh). The fertile river valleys provided the agricultural crops, including different grains and fruits that fed the cities and supported a wide network of trade. Experts do not yet have the evidence to explain who ruled these cities, but priests and traders were clearly very important in Indus society.

Then, about four thousand years ago, the Indus Valley civilization suddenly collapsed. The reasons for this are still unclear. The river valleys, which provided the Indus peoples with their wealth, may also have been the cause of their downfall. They suffered from periods of flooding, drought, and rivers changing course. Catastrophic floods or farmland turning to desert may have finally destroyed their way of life. Some experts also believe that they were weakened by

Archaeological excavations at the ancient city of Mohenjo Daro have revealed that its people knew a great deal about city planning and engineering.

Collapse of Indus Valley civilization	Aryan peoples begin to move into Indus and Ganga Valleys; begin to settle and trade; Aryan absorb ideas and beliefs from Dravidian peoples; beginnings of Hinduism	Rise of independent Aryan states, including Magadha
ca. 2000 B.C.E.	**ca. 1500 B.C.E.**	**ca. 500 B.C.E.**

Mohenjo Daro and Harappa

Many artifacts have been unearthed, which tell us about people's daily lives and work. They include pottery figures and carved stone seals (a closure for something, such as a package or a container), which were probably used by traders. These objects show wild and domesticated animals, ordinary people, priests, gods, and goddesses. Inscriptions on the seals show that the Indus people had a system of writing, but no expert has yet been able to interpret the script.

One of the many beautiful artifacts found at Mohenjo Daro is this seal carved from soapstone. The animal is the mythical unicorn, often shown on Indus seals.

raids — or by conquest — from Aryan (AHR-yuhn) peoples who came in from the north.

The Coming of the Aryans

From around 1500 B.C.E., groups of Indo-European peoples began to spread from the north into the Indus and Ganga Valleys. They became known as Aryans. At first they were seminomadic and kept cattle. Over the centuries they began to farm and to settle in villages, and then to trade and develop towns along the Ganga River. By about 500 B.C.E, several independent states had developed, and the most powerful of these was Magadha (MEH-guh-duh). As the Aryan way of life spread, it absorbed ideas and beliefs from the Dravidian peoples. From this came Hinduism, the oldest of the great world religions.

There is almost no archaeological evidence on this period of Indian history. The main sources of information are oral and written: what we know about Aryan religion and society comes from the Vedas (VAE-duhs), the Upanishads, the *Mahabharata* (mah-huhb-RAH-tuh), the *Ramayana* (rah-muh-YAH-nuh), and the Hindu myths of creation known as the Puranas.

The Vedas contain thousands of sacred hymns in Sanskrit (SAN-skriht), an ancient

Alexander the Great invades India; driven out by Chandragupta, a prince of Magadha. Chandragupta founds Mauryan Empire

Under Ashoka, ruler of the Mauryan Empire, almost all of India is united; Buddhism spreads through India and to other Asian countries

327–325 B.C.E.

269–232 B.C.E.

This miniature from the Mahabharata *was made in the sixteenth century, in the Mogul style, some two thousand years after the* Mahabharata *was first recited.*

language of India. These hymns were learned by heart and chanted by the priests. The Vedas describe the main religious traditions of Hinduism, including the origins of the caste system, the divisions of Indian society that still exist to this day. The Upanishads, the last of the Vedas, provided explanations and interpretations of the main Vedic texts. The *Mahabharata* and the *Ramayana* contain many different tales, of power struggles and wars, of undying love, of gods and goddesses appearing in human form, and of the final triumph of good over evil. Most of the stories in these epic poems are imaginary, but historians today believe that they grew out of real historical events in ancient India.

The Mauryan Age

In the sixth century B.C.E. northwest India became part of the Persian Empire. Persia (present-day Iran) was later conquered and absorbed into the vast empire of the Macedonian (Ma-seh-DOE-nee-uhn) Alexander the Great. Between 327 B.C.E. and 325 B.C.E. Alexander invaded India, but he was finally driven out by Chandragupta, a prince of Magadha. Chandragupta founded the Mauryan (MAWR-yuhn) Empire and brought all of northern India under his rule. During the reign of his grandson, Ashoka, all of India except for the far south and the lands to the east of the Brahmaputra River was united.

Under Ashoka, India became famous for its learning and culture. Trade flourished and Buddhism became the leading religion.

Gupta dynasty rules northern India; culture, religion, and trade flourish; Hinduism becomes leading religion	Decline and break up of Gupta Empire; several small kingdoms, often at war	Muslim armies plunder Hindu temples; first Muslim kingdom, the Delhi Sultanate, is established in India
300s–500s c.e.	**500s–900s**	**900s–1100s**

Ashoka, Ruler of the Mauryan Empire

Ashoka (269–232 B.C.E.) was probably the greatest ruler in ancient India. After many successful early conquests, however, he became sickened by war and bloodshed. He began to preach nonviolence and religious tolerance, and encouraged people to convert to Buddhism. During his reign Buddhism spread through much of India and to other Asian countries, and it became established as a world religion. Yet after Ashoka's death, the Mauryan Empire fell apart, and Buddhism began to decline.

A lasting legacy of Ashoka's reign was the inscriptions he had carved on pillars and rocks throughout the empire. These inscriptions explained his ideas on religion, good government, and how people should behave toward one another. Ashoka also tried to improve everyday life in his empire: he set up hospitals for people and animals, built roads, made the laws more fair, and traveled widely to meet his subjects.

The "Classical Age"

After the break up of the Mauryan Empire, Indian unity came to an end. For nearly five hundred years, different invaders came in from the north, while several smaller states rose and fell. Then, during the fourth century C.E., a new Indian dynasty came to power in Magadha. The Gupta (GOOP-tuh) dynasty ruled most of northern India for nearly two hundred years. Under Chandragupta I and his grandson Chandragupta II, Indian culture, religion, and trade once again flourished. This became known as the "Classical Age" for the achievements in literature, science, astronomy, education, art, and architecture. Buddhism and Jainism were important religions, but Hinduism now became the leading Indian faith. Many Hindu temples were built, while artists created beautiful carvings and paintings of Hindu gods and goddesses.

The Gupta Empire was weakened by raiding Hun tribesmen from central Asia and broke up during the sixth century C.E. It rose again in the seventh century, but it then broke up into small warring kingdoms until the Muslims arrived in India nearly four hundred years later.

Southern India

The Dravidian peoples of southern India felt the influence of northern Indo-Aryan culture: Hinduism became the strongest religion, and Sanskrit became the language of learning. In other ways, though, Dravidian life and culture were relatively untouched. Southern languages, such as Tamil, Telugu, Malayalam (mah-luh-YAH-luhm), and Kannada (KAH-nuh-duh), and literature continued to flourish.

Over the centuries the Dravidians developed strong trading links with Greece, Rome, Southeast Asia, and Portugal. These

Muslim Sultans conquer most of India	Hindu Empire of Vijayanagar flourishes in South India	Portuguese explorer Vasco da Gama lands at Kozhikode, Kerala, in southwest India	Portuguese capture Goa
1100s–1300s	1300s–1500s	1498	1510

links helped ancient Dravidian, Hindu, and Buddhist culture to spread to much of Southeast Asia. Wealth from this trade also helped to establish southern kingdoms such as Chola (CHOE-luh) and Pandya (PAHND-yuh). These smaller, local kingdoms were often raided and defeated by the more powerful north, but they were not wiped out.

Muslim India

As the kingdoms and empires of India rose and fell, Islam was beginning to spread through the Middle East and central Asia. From the tenth century onward, Muslim armies began frequent, destructive raids to plunder the treasures of Hindu temples. At the end of the twelfth century, the first Muslim kingdom, the Delhi Sultanate, was established in India. Successive rulers conquered almost all of India, including the south. The Sultans were powerful and were effective military leaders, but their rule was often violent and unstable. The Delhi Sultanate began to weaken from the fourteenth century onward.

Meanwhile, in the south, the Hindu Empire of Vijayanagar (veezh-uh-YAH-nuh-gahr) rose in the fourteenth century and flourished as a center of trade and learning for over two hundred years.

In 1526 Babur, a Turkic ruler from Afghanistan, invaded India from the northwest. His small, highly trained army defeated the huge forces of the Delhi Sultan, and Babur became the first of the great Mogul (MOE-gool) emperors. Babur's conquests were consolidated by

his grandson, Akbar, who expanded the Mogul Empire throughout much of India. Akbar ruled India for nearly fifty years, from 1556 to 1605.

Under Akbar's successors, Jahangir and Shah Jahan, the Mogul Empire was at its peak. India had a stable government and economic success. The court of the Mogul emperors attracted leading writers and

This exquisite Mogul miniature, from the Akbar-Nama, *was painted in the last years of Akbar's rule. It shows Akbar traveling by boat on an expedition to the eastern provinces.*

Turkic ruler Babur invades India; defeats Delhi Sultan and becomes first of the great Mogul emperors	Akbar expands Mogul Empire throughout much of India; encourages religious tolerance; builds beautiful palaces, mosques, and forts
1526	**1556–1605**

Akbar, the Greatest of the Mogul Emperors

Although he never learned to read or write, Akbar was a man of great wisdom and understanding. He was a powerful military leader who fought many battles, but he also established efficient government throughout his empire.

Akbar understood the importance of working with those he conquered. He employed many Hindus in his government, and he banned the head tax on non-Muslims. He encouraged religious tolerance, celebrated Hindu festivals, and debated with religious leaders from different faiths.

Akbar left a great legacy in Mogul architecture. Beautiful palaces, mosques (MAWSKS), and forts were built during his reign. He built a new capital at Fatehpur Sikri (FAH-tuh-poor SEE-kree), where a Muslim holy man had prophesied the birth of Akbar's sons.

Although poor water supplies meant that Akbar's new capital at Fatehpur Sikri was soon deserted, many of its beautiful sandstone buildings remain intact to this day.

artists, as well as visitors from Europe, who were amazed by its wealth and magnificence. Mogul art and architecture reached new heights of beauty in the bejeweled Peacock Throne of Shah Jahan—but above all in the Taj Mahal (TAHZH muh-HAWL), the tomb he built when his beloved wife died. Shah Jahan's reign was also a time of extravagance and corruption, and of growing intolerance toward the followers of other faiths.

Religious intolerance reached its height under Aurangzeb, Shah Jahan's son, and the last of the powerful Mogul rulers. He seized power after murdering his older brothers and imprisoning his father. He destroyed Hindu temples and persecuted other faiths, especially the Jains and the Sikhs. Although Aurangzeb expanded the geographical limits of the Mogul Empire, there were many uprisings against his rule. After his death in 1707, the weakened Mogul Empire began to fall apart.

Mogul Empire reaches its height under the emperors Jahangir and Shah Jahan; Taj Mahal built; growing corruption and religious intolerance	Rule of Aurangzeb; persecution of other faiths; uprisings against his rule weaken Mogul Empire
1605–1658	**1658–1707**

This nineteenth-century lithograph, The Breakfast, shows a couple keeping up British traditions in India. In spite of the hot climate, they are dressed in formal Victorian clothes.

European Explorers and Traders

Europeans knew of the great riches of India and other Asian lands. They wanted direct trade links with the East, but they were hindered by conflicts with Muslim powers in Middle Eastern lands. So they began to seek a sea route to India.

The first European to make the sea voyage to India was Portuguese explorer Vasco da Gama. He landed at Kozhikode (Calicut), Kerala, in southwest India in 1498. In 1510 the Portuguese captured Goa, from where they controlled much of the sea trade for over one hundred years.

From the early seventeenth century, there was fierce competition between European powers to take control of trade in the East. As Portuguese power declined, the British, Dutch, and French set up trading companies and established trading stations in India. They bought spices, cotton, silk, calico, and indigo.

During the eighteenth century, India had no single strong ruler and was politically unstable. The Mogul rulers had lost their authority, and there were many revolts among the Hindus. The British and the French fought each other for control of India's trade, each making alliances with different Indian rulers.

The British East India Company

The East India Company, with its own army, became very powerful. In 1757 the company's army, led by Robert Clive, defeated the powerful Nabob Sirajud-Daulah of Bengal at the Battle of Plassey. This battle marked the end of French influence in India and the beginnings of British imperial rule. By the early nineteenth century the East India Company ruled most of India on behalf of the British government.

Indian resentment of foreign rule finally exploded in 1857 when Indian troops in the East India Company's army mutinied. The uprising became known as the Indian

India politically unstable; Mogul Empire in decline; British and French fight to control India's trade; British East India Company becomes very powerful

Army of East India Company defeats Nabob of Bengal at Battle of Plassey, marking beginnings of British imperial rule of India

1700s

1757

An engraving showing a battle between British and Indian soldiers during the Indian Mutiny. Brutality on both sides left a lasting legacy of resentment.

Mutiny, or Sepoy Rebellion. It spread through north India and lasted for nearly two years before the British finally crushed the rebels. In 1858 the British government abolished the East India Company and took direct control of the subcontinent.

The British Raj

In 1876 Queen Victoria was crowned Empress of India, and British power over India was complete. About two-thirds of the country was ruled directly by Great Britain; the rest by Indian rulers. There were more than five hundred "princely" states. The princes swore loyalty to the British queen, and in return they had land and titles. In reality they had little power.

This was the Age of Imperialism, when Great Britain and other European powers were building empires in Africa and Asia. The British wanted to run India cheaply but efficiently. They also needed raw materials, such as cotton, for their factories back in Great Britain and markets abroad for the goods produced in those factories. To do this they began to improve communications in India: they built railroads, bridges, and roads; they introduced postal services and electric telegraph lines. They brought in basic Western education, mostly through Christian mission schools. Ironically, those improvements also helped to spread nationalist ideas: Indians could now travel more easily and communicate more effectively with each other.

British East India Company rules most of India, on behalf of British government	Indian Mutiny spreads through north India; British government abolishes East India Company and takes direct control of Indian Empire	Queen Victoria is crowned Empress of India; "British Raj" at its height
Early 1800s	**1857–1858**	**1876**

Rich and Poor under the Raj

India has always had extremes of wealth and poverty, but these seemed even more glaring under the British Raj. Many of the princes, stripped of real power and responsibility, nevertheless enjoyed enormous wealth. They lived extravagantly, spending vast amounts on luxury goods. Some princes even ate from plates made of gold.

The British did little to improve the lives of ordinary Indians. Many lived in great poverty. Poor farmers found it difficult to compete with large-scale farms, which grew cash crops such as cotton, tea, and indigo, while craft workers could not compete with cheap goods from British factories. Taxation also impoverished them. Crops often failed because of floods and droughts, and there were frequent famines. In 1866, 1.5 million people died during a famine in Orissa.

When the British first came to India, many settled in local communities, married Indian wives, and traded and worked as equals with Indians, but by the time of the British Raj (RAHZH), they had come to believe that the Indian way of life, its history and culture, were inferior to their own. In ruling India, they had a "mission to civilize." They kept themselves apart, living in separate areas, and socializing only with other British people.

Toward Independence

By the late nineteenth century, Indian nationalism was growing. India's first national political party, the Indian National Congress, was formed in 1885. Its youthful leaders were mostly British educated and middle class, and they wanted Indians to rule India.

The British began to include Indians in the administration, but at the same time they introduced political changes and repressive laws that inflamed Indian public opinion. In 1905 the large, densely populated region of Bengal was divided into two provinces so that it could be ruled more efficiently. The British did this without consulting the Bengali people, who expressed their anger in street demonstrations and newspaper articles. The Indian National Congress began a movement known as Swadeshi (swuh-DAE-shee), which encouraged people to use locally made Indian goods and to boycott British-made goods. Conflict between the British and the nationalists led to violence, terrorism, and the frequent imprisonment of Congress leaders.

Many Indians fought—and died—alongside the British in World War I (1914–1918). Yet in 1919, to control increasingly violent opposition to British rule, the government introduced the Rowlatts Act, which took away many civil rights of Indians and allowed imprisonment without trial. This was followed by the Amritsar (uhm-RIHT-suhr) Massacre (1919), in which over four hundred peaceful protestors were killed by British troops.

India's first national political party, the Indian National Congress, is formed and campaigns for Indians to rule India	British divide Bengal into two provinces; Indian protests and demonstrations; Indian National Congress begins Swadeshi, boycotting British-made goods
1885	**1905**

This artwork depicts King George V traveling to Delhi in 1911 for a great durbar *(a formal reception) to celebrate his accession to the British throne.*

Popular feeling against the British increased support for the Indian National Congress, which now had a following throughout India. Under leaders such as Jawaharlal Nehru and Mahatma Gandhi, Indians refused to cooperate with the government, and the British began to accept that, at some time, they would have to grant India independence.

However, Indian Muslims were becoming increasingly fearful of domination by Hindus, who made up the majority of the population. The Muslim League, led by Muhammad Ali Jinnah, began to argue for a separate Muslim state. This led to violence between Hindus and Muslims.

In 1935 the Government of India Act gave India greater self-government. After World War II (1939–1945), the Congress Party stepped up its "Quit India" campaign, demanding immediate and full independence. The situation became increasingly dangerous, with anti-British riots and tensions between Hindus and Muslims threatening to erupt into civil war. Congress and the Muslim League failed to agree on the future makeup of

British introduce Rowlatts Act, allowing imprisonment without trial; over four hundred peaceful protestors killed in the Amritsar Massacre	Indian demands for independence increase; Congress Party has support throughout India; rise of Muslim League, led by Muhammad Ali Jinnah
1919	**1920s–1930s**

Gandhi gained many followers from among the poorest in Indian society. He fought for their rights, calling them Harijans—"children of God."

Mahatma Gandhi

Mahatma Gandhi (1869–1948) was a religious and political leader whose beliefs and actions inspired millions of Indians. He campaigned against British rule and was imprisoned several times. Gandhi insisted that all actions must be nonviolent, and his policy of boycotting British goods, schools, and courts was highly successful. In 1930 he led the famous salt march in protest against the British monopoly on salt production and the high taxes they charged on its sale. Gandhi and thousands of followers walked for nearly a month to reach the sea. They boiled seawater to extract the salt: a symbolic act of defiance that sent a powerful message to the British government.

The Mahatma (muh-HAHT-muh), meaning "great soul," lived a simple and devout life. He encouraged Indians to revive their village industries and tried to bring peace to Hindu and Muslim communities. A Hindu fanatic assassinated him in 1948.

independent India. In 1947 the British Governor-General announced the partition of British India into the independent nations of India and Pakistan, with the latter divided between East and West Pakistan (see BANGLADESH).

The Nehru Years (1947–1964)

In August 1947 India regained full independence, with the Congress party in power and Jawaharlal Nehru as its first prime minister. In 1950 India became a democratic republic, with a new written constitution. The first elections were held in 1952.

Government of India Act gives India greater self-government	"Quit India" campaign; anti-British riots; rising tensions between Hindus and Muslims	Partition of British India into independent nations of India and Pakistan
1935	**1940s**	**1947**

The hasty partition of India and Pakistan along religious lines left unresolved problems. There were large Muslim minorities in India, while Sikh and Hindu minorities found themselves marooned in Islamic Pakistan. As conflict intensified, millions of refugees tried to flee to safety across the India-Pakistan borders. An estimated half a million people died in bitter religious attacks.

In spite of these problems, the Indian government, led by Nehru, began a

Jawaharlal Nehru in 1954 at a reception held to celebrate his 66th birthday. Here he releases one of sixty-six white pigeons, symbols of peace, prosperity, and freedom.

The Question of Kashmir

Upon independence, most of the "princely" states chose to join India. In the far north a Hindu maharajah ruled the large, mostly Muslim state of Jammu and Kashmir. The majority of Kashmir's people wished to join with Pakistan, but the maharajah, under pressure from both countries, finally decided that Kashmir should be part of India. War over Kashmir broke out between India and Pakistan in 1948, after which the region was divided between the two countries.

Muslim separatists in Indian Kashmir have continued to fight for an independent state or for union with Pakistan. Other Kashmiris wish to remain part of India. Despite United Nations attempts to bring peace to this region, simmering hostilities between India and Pakistan over the future of Kashmir continue to this day.

program to modernize India and to fight against poverty and inequality. There were reforms in the law to give rights to women, to the poor, and to lower-caste Hindus. There was rapid development in industry and in agriculture, and new research and scientific centers were set up. India was transformed into the largest parliamentary democracy in the world.

India becomes democratic republic; Nehru is first prime minister; serious conflicts between Hindus and Muslims in India and Pakistan; war between India and Pakistan over Kashmir in 1948	Indira Gandhi is prime minister	India defeats Pakistan in wars over Kashmir and Bangladesh
1947–1964	**1966–1984**	**1971**

The Gandhi Years (1966–1991)

Nehru died in 1964, and two years later his daughter, Indira Gandhi (no relation to Mahatma Gandhi), became prime minister. She continued her father's ambitious program of reforms, including nationalizing India's large banks. In the early years, her strong leadership was popular, especially in 1971 when India defeated Pakistan in wars in Kashmir and Bangladesh (then East Pakistan). Ten million refugees fled into India during Bangladesh's bid for independence from Pakistan. In 1974 India joined the world's nuclear powers when it exploded its first nuclear device.

Indira Gandhi was India's first—and to date, only—female prime minister. Her family dominated Indian politics for many years.

But Indira Gandhi's growing abuse of power led to much opposition. Her campaign against poverty went sour: poor families were evicted from slum homes and many suffered forced sterilization in an attempt to control the ever-growing population. In 1975 Indira declared a state of emergency and imprisoned thousands of her opponents. She lost power after the 1977 elections, but she was reelected in 1980. Increasing conflicts within India reached new heights in 1984 when the army stormed the Sikh's most holy shrine, the Golden Temple at Amritsar, killing many Sikh militants inside. Indira was assassinated that year by her Sikh bodyguards.

Rajiv Gandhi, her eldest son, became prime minister. Rajiv sought to meet the demands of India's different regions and religious and ethnic groups. He worked to modernize and develop the economy, but political unrest continued, and in 1991 Rajiv was assassinated by a Tamil suicide bomber from Sri Lanka (sree LAHN-kuh).

The 1990s

The Congress Party and the Nehru-Gandhi reign had dominated the government of India for over forty years. In the 1990s the

India explodes first nuclear device	Indira Gandhi declares state of emergency	Army storms Sikh Golden Temple at Amritsar; Indira Gandhi is assassinated by Sikh bodyguards	Rajiv Gandhi is prime minister; he is assassinated in 1991 by Tamil suicide bomber
1974	**1975**	**1984**	**1984–1991**

Gandhi era was over and Congress was less powerful. There were frequent changes of government and leadership, short-lived coalitions between different parties, and questions about corruption among high-level politicians.

The 1990s also saw a rise in Hindu nationalism and the growing popularity of the Bharatiya Janata Party (BJP), a conservative Hindu nationalist political party. Tensions between Hindus and Muslims came to a head in 1993 when Hindu nationalists destroyed a mosque at Ayodhya (uh-YOED-jah), claiming it to be the birthplace of Rama, hero of the *Ramayana*, and the site of a Hindu temple.

Both India and Pakistan tested several nuclear devices during the 1990s, raising fears that conflict in the region could lead to the use of nuclear weapons.

India in the New Millennium

The opening of the new millennium saw the birth of India's billionth citizen—a baby girl named Astha. India is still the world's largest democracy and a major world power, but rapid population growth, inequality and poverty, and continuing regional and religious tensions present many challenges for the future.

Conflict between Hindus and Muslims exploded once more in 2002 with religious riots in the state of Gujarat (goozh-uh-RAHT). More than two thousand people died, while thousands of Muslims became refugees in their own land as militant Hindus drove them from their homes and villages.

Relations with Pakistan remained tense, with both powers testing nuclear missiles and unrest in Kashmir continuing. At the end of 2001, a militant Kashmiri suicide squad attacked the parliament in New Delhi, hitting at the heart of India's democracy.

Peoples and Languages

The origins of the many different peoples of India are complex. For many centuries peoples of different ethnic groups and cultures have come into the region, either to conquer or to settle. The mixing of these groups with existing peoples has resulted in the mosaic of languages and cultures that is India today.

There are, however, two broad groups of peoples and languages that dominate: the Indo-Aryans in the north and east, who make up approximately 72 percent of the population, and Dravidians in the south, who make up about 25 percent. Northern languages developed from Sanskrit, spoken by the Aryans, who came in from the north. Southern languages developed from those spoken by the earlier Dravidian peoples. They use different alphabets from northern languages, such as Hindi. A person speaking a southern Indian language often cannot communicate with a northern language speaker.

The Indian constitution recognizes fourteen official regional languages, and the boundaries of several of India's states are determined by language. The most important language is Hindi, which is spoken by nearly half the population.

Frequent changes of government and leadership; rise in Hindu nationalism and BJP party; growing tensions between Hindu nationalists and Muslims; both India and Pakistan become nuclear powers, leading to increased tension in the region	India's billionth citizen is born
1990s	**2000**

Minority Peoples

Minority peoples make up approximately 8 percent of India's population. Scattered throughout India, there are more than five hundred communities that the government recognizes as Scheduled Tribes. Their ethnic origins are different from most Indians, and often from each other: they have distinctive physical features and languages. Many of their languages have no script or have borrowed one from another language.

Minority peoples often live in remote, hilly areas. They are found in the northeast along the Himalayas and in the hills of central India, in Madhya Pradesh, and Orissa. In some states they make up nearly 90 percent of the population, in others only a small percentage. Larger groups include the Gonds, Santals, and Nagas.

The unique languages and cultures of the minority peoples have long been under threat. As Scheduled Tribes, they now have special benefits to protect their way of life.

Women from the Banjara people in Andhra Pradesh, central India. They wear traditional dress, embroidered with small mirrors. Many Banjara women wear jewelry.

However, in south India the main language is Tamil, and few people speak Hindi. English has a special status as an international language and is widely used in business, government, and higher education. There are also several hundred local languages and dialects, which are spoken in different parts of India.

India has a rich tradition of both spoken and written literature in northern languages such as Sanskrit, Bengali, Urdu, and Hindi and in the Dravidian languages of the south, including Tamil, Kannada, Telugu, and Malayalam. There are eleven different Indian scripts.

Economy and Resources

India has many and varied natural resources. It has vast areas of land for farming (nearly 52 percent of the land, compared to 19 percent in the United States) and the waters of its great rivers, the Indian Ocean, and the Arabian Sea. It has large deposits of fossil fuels such as coal, oil, and natural gas. Its mineral

186

resources include iron ore, bauxite, manganese, and aluminum.

The Indian economy is a complex mix of the traditional and the modern. About two-thirds of the population continues to live by farming in rural communities. Yet India also has highly developed modern industries: today it is the tenth most industrialized country in the world.

Most farming is small scale, with farmers growing enough food to feed their families and perhaps a few cash crops to sell. During the 1970s the "green revolution" modernized Indian farming methods. The government encouraged farmers to grow higher-yielding crops and to use irrigation, machines, and fertilizers so that the country could become self-sufficient in food and escape the terrible famines of the past. The main food crops include rice, wheat, tea, sugarcane, and beans. Sorghum, corn, fruits, vegetables, and spices are also grown. Important non-food crops include oilseed, cotton, tobacco, and jute. Farmers often keep a few animals such as cows and buffalo, which they use mostly for plowing or milk, and goats and sheep for their wool. Fishing is an important livelihood for people who live on the coast or near rivers. The forests of India provide wood for fuel, as well as food and medicine from fruits, nuts, bark, and leaves.

India has very large manufacturing industries. The most important of these produce textiles, iron, and steel. Other industries include chemicals, transport equipment, machines, printing, and publishing, as well as the processing of food and other agricultural crops. India's great movie industry and its tourism are growing rapidly, providing both wealth and employment. India's computer software industry is now a world leader, the main base for which is Bangalore, a modern city in the south known as India's Silicon Valley.

A vast network of roads and railroads connects the towns and cities of India. For longer journeys, people travel by bus or by train, or, if they can afford it, by air. For shorter distances, especially in rural areas, many people still rely on bullock (a young bull) or horse-drawn carts to transport themselves and their goods.

A steam train in the Nilgiri Hills, Tamil Nadu, southern India. India has one of the most extensive rail networks in the world.

A rickshaw driver in Kolkata. City roads overflow with all forms of transportation, including cars, bicycles, scooters, rickshaws, and buses.

family businesses provide more employment than large-scale industry, but in some ways the poor are more vulnerable than ever: large farms growing cash crops are replacing food production, while small farm plots are being lost to mining, industry, and large-scale development projects. Millions still lack decent housing, access to safe water, proper sanitation, and basic education. Today, the country is

India also has an extensive communications network. There is widespread use of telephones. Many people have access to radio and to both state-owned and satellite television. It is estimated that television now reaches nearly half the population. There is a flourishing newspaper and magazine industry. India has a free press—which is often very critical of its politicians. The number of internet users is small, but growing rapidly. At the beginning of the millennium, there were less than five million users; by 2005 there are expected to be more than thirty million.

Rich and Poor in Modern India

The growth of India's economy and increasing industrialization has brought great wealth to some. Today, India also has a large and successful middle class. Small

The Narmada Valley Dams

The Narmada (nuhr-MAH-duh) is one of India's largest rivers, flowing through several states in western India. There have been various projects to build dams along the river valley to provide large amounts of energy and water. The most recent project—to build several thousand dams of different sizes, including thirty large dams—has created huge controversy in India. It will flood farms and villages and displace many thousands of people.

Opponents argue that the project will deprive large numbers of very poor families, mostly minority peoples or dalits (DAH-lihtz: "untouchables"), of their homes, their work, and their communities. Smaller projects, they argue, are less damaging to local communities and to the environment.

Supporters say that the project will provide water and electricity for industry, farms, and homes, and bring wealth to an underdeveloped region of India.

188

able to feed itself, yet many rural dwellers are undernourished.

Debt is often a problem for the poor. If the harvest fails, or if there is little work, they may have to borrow money to buy food or to pay the owner of the land they farm or the landlord of the rooms they rent. Moneylenders charge very high rates of interest, which means that families may struggle for years to get out of debt.

Another problem that faces Indian society is child labor. India has the largest number of working children in the world. Statistics are very unreliable, but figures range from sixty to over one hundred million working children; most are to be found in rural areas, helping their families on the farm, in the home, or learning craft skills.

In the cities children often work in factories. Many poor families rely on the income their children can bring in. Child labor, especially in factories, means that employers can pay less and have the power to control — or even beat — the children. Some children are bonded laborers, forced into service because of a family debt. Some child workers have recently begun to organize themselves to demand an end to child labor.

Education

In 1991, according to the national census, 52 percent of Indians could read and write. Ten years later, in 2001, the literacy rate was estimated at just over 70 percent. The numbers vary greatly from state to state: in Kerala State, in southwest India, for example, nine out of every ten adults are literate. In most states, however, women's literacy is much lower than men's.

The different stages of elementary and high school education also vary according to state. However, most children start school at the age of five or six. After five years of elementary education, they spend three years in middle school, followed by two years of high school. Some pupils then go on to two years of higher secondary education. Education is free, but it is not compulsory throughout India. Children usually learn their main subjects in their mother tongue or the language of their region. In most states they also have to learn Hindi and English.

Higher education in India includes more than two hundred universities and over

Some children, like these, have begun to demand an end to child labor, voicing their opinions and views at marches like this one, a global march against child labor in April 1998.

five thousand colleges, teaching arts, science, and technical subjects. There are several specialist institutions that are leading centers in their subject area, including management and technology, and three world-class academies of science in Delhi, Bangalore, and Allahabad (AHL-uh-huh-bahd).

The state governments provide most education, but different types of private education are also available. Wealthier parents often send their children to fee-paying schools, which can offer a higher standard of education than the state school system. There are also religious schools, including Christian church and missionary schools and Islamic *madrasas* (muh-DRAH-suhs). Madrasas are attached to many neighborhood mosques and teach children about Islamic beliefs and practices.

India faces major challenges in its aim to provide universal elementary and high school education. The rapidly growing population places heavy demands on the educational system. Funding for schools, especially in rural areas, is spread thin, and many schools are short of teachers, books, and basic necessities such as drinking water and bathrooms. In some areas schools operate a shift system to help overcome a shortage of teachers and classroom space, with some children attending only in the mornings, others in the afternoons.

Indian parents place a high value on education, but many poor families rely on their children to help in the home, on the farm, or in the family business. For this reason, many children may be enrolled in schools but attend infrequently or not at all, or they may drop out before they complete their elementary schooling. Although more emphasis is now given to educating girls, the majority of parents still value their sons' education above that of daughters. The children of middle and upper class families, who can afford better education, are much more likely to complete school and go on to higher education.

Outside the formal education system, the tradition of handing down skills and knowledge from parent to child remains strong. In small families throughout India,

Children at a village elementary school in Andhra Pradesh, central India. Their lesson takes place outdoors: many rural schools do not have the funds for adequate classrooms.

Education and Learning in Ancient India

The achievements of early Indian scholars are remarkable. Hindu, Buddhist, and, later, Muslim scholars studied in many different fields, including mathematics, astronomy, medicine, religion, literature, and art. Early Indian astronomers studied the solar system and the movements of stars. In 400 C.E. the astronomer Bhaskaracharya calculated that it took 365.258 days for the Earth to orbit the Sun. Mathematical scholars developed algebra, trigonometry, calculus, the decimal system, and the concept of zero. From the time of the Indus Valley civilization, the work of Indian scientists and mathematicians was also put to practical use in irrigation, town planning, architecture, and textile production.

The first followers of Buddha established a long tradition of learning. In Buddhist universities, education was free and anyone could attend. The most famous Buddhist university was at Nalanda (Nah-luhn-DUH), in northeast India. It flourished for several hundred years and drew students from throughout Asia.

a father may teach his son the skills of, for example, blacksmithing, tailoring, fishing, farming, or running the family business. A mother will teach her children about their religion, for example, Hindu worship and stories from the Hindu epics, as well as practical skills in making things such as baskets, pots, and embroidery work.

In recent years the Indian government has also placed great emphasis on adult literacy, running national campaigns to teach villagers, especially women, how to read and write, and also on how to learn new practical skills to improve the quality of their lives.

The eighteenth-century observatory in Jaipur, in northwest India. It was built by Maharaja Jai Singh II, a warrior-ruler whose greatest passion was astronomy.

Health

Compared with countries in the West, life expectancy in India is fairly low. Yet, in less than one hundred years, it has risen dramatically—from an average of just over twenty years to just under sixty-three years in 2001.

191

In the past many babies and small children died because they were undernourished and too weak to resist infectious diseases. In the later years of the twentieth century, more children lived to adulthood. Farming methods improved, and families had more food to eat. National and local government programs were introduced to improve supplies of safe drinking water and sanitation facilities.

Nationwide immunization programs have helped to protect people, especially children, from infectious diseases, such as smallpox, polio, and measles. There have also been intensive programs to reduce— and, it is hoped, eventually to wipe out— major diseases such as tuberculosis, leprosy, and guinea worm disease. Health services have expanded throughout the country. Today there are many more doctors, nurses, and rural health workers than there were at independence in 1947. Health promotion campaigns help to teach families about staying healthy, giving children a good start in life, and about family planning.

As people are living longer, however, overpopulation has become the major problem facing India today. This in turn places a strain on health facilities, especially in rural areas. Many millions of Indians still live in poverty and are undernourished. Many, above all in the villages, do not have safe drinking water or proper sanitation. This in turn makes them vulnerable to infections and disease.

With the majority of families living in overcrowded conditions, infectious diseases can spread rapidly. Mosquito bites bring diseases such as malaria and filariasis (a disease caused by a small parasitic worm that infects the blood). Tuberculosis is still a major problem. Early in 2002 there was an outbreak of pneumonic plague, a highly infectious disease that can kill within one day if it is not treated immediately.

Indians are also suffering an increase of modern lifestyle diseases, such as cancer, heart disease, and diabetes. More young people are smoking, and families who have higher incomes are eating more fast food and exercising less. People's health is also suffering through air pollution from motor vehicles and unclean industries in the cities and from the heavy use of pesticides and weed killers on crops in rural areas. Health experts also fear that AIDS will soon become a major problem in India. There are no accurate figures at present, but estimates suggest that about one million Indians have AIDS, and as many as five million may be HIV-positive.

Health-care facilities, and the amount of money spent on them, vary

In a village in Madhya Pradesh, central India, a health worker gives advice to mothers on healthy foods for themselves and their children.

The Neem Tree – the Rural Indian's "Village Pharmacy"

Indians have appreciated the usefulness of the neem tree for thousands of years. Ancient Vedic texts mention many different uses of neem in all aspects of daily life.

An evergreen tropical tree, the neem grows in many Indian villages. Almost all parts – the leaves, bark, fruit, and seeds – are used in different ways: as medicine, as insect repellent, as an organic insecticide on food crops, as a source of oil to light lamps, and as part of religious ceremonies. Neem twigs are even used for brushing teeth.

Ayurvedic practitioners use neem extracts both to prevent and treat disease. Recent research in India and in Western countries has shown that the neem has special properties that may strengthen the immune system, offering possible protection and treatment of HIV and AIDS.

many private doctors trained in Western medicine and also many who practice traditional Indian medicine. The most widely used traditional practice is *Ayurveda* (ie-yuhr-VAE-duh), an ancient system of Hindu medicine. The word *Ayurveda* means "science of life" and is about living a healthy, balanced life as well as treating diseases. Ayurvedic principles state that a person becomes sick when the body is out of balance. To achieve balance, Ayurvedic practitioners focus on diet and lifestyle. They use medicines made from herbs, plants, and minerals. *Unani* (oo-NAH-nee) is the traditional Muslim system of medicine, which also treats the whole person. It uses mostly herbal treatments.

India's Minority Peoples: A Threatened Way of Life?

India's minority groups always had different lifestyles and cultures from the majority of the population. Many have traditionally lived as hunters and gatherers, relying on the wild game and the fruits, seeds, and roots of the forests. The forests are also a source of wild honey and medicines from different plants. Some minority peoples also grow crops, but their traditional way of farming is different from the more intensive, permanent use of land of most Indian farmers. They practice slash-and-burn cultivation, suited to the forests and hilly areas where they live. Farmers cut down the trees and burn the vegetation to clear the land. They grow crops for two or three seasons, then move on to new land when the soil becomes exhausted. This type of shifting cultivation is becoming less sustainable as Indian forests are cut down for lumber.

greatly from state to state. Primary health centers are important, especially in rural areas, but are often short of skilled medical workers, who prefer to work in towns. State governments try to involve the community in health and family welfare programs, including family planning and health education. There is particular concern about women and girls, whose health and general welfare may be seen as less important than that of men and boys.

More and more Indians, especially among the growing middle class, are turning to private health care. There are

Most minority peoples live in small communities. They rarely own land, but share it among themselves. In thickly

Living by hunting and gathering and by shifting cultivation means that in many ways minority peoples are freer than those living in cities.

forested areas, they roam freely over large distances, taking only what they need. Many communities do not have powerful leaders or headmen; instead they may have a council of elders who make decisions and punish wrongdoers.

Development and population growth have seriously threatened the minority peoples' way of life. Other Indians have moved onto their land to farm; loggers have cut down huge areas of forest; and state governments have taken land for large projects, such as mining and hydroelectric dams, often without compensation. New roads and improved communications have made these areas, especially in central India, less remote than they once were.

Large numbers of minority peoples have abandoned their traditional lifestyle. Some find work as landless laborers or in the towns. Some have become absorbed into Hinduism and the caste system, usually into the lowest castes or the dalits (untouchables). Many Hindus still look at minority peoples as backward. In the more remote, underdeveloped northeast, many minority peoples have converted to Christianity.

In recent years organizations have been formed to protect their way of life. Largely as a result of their campaigning, the Indian government passed the Tribal Self-rule Act in 1996. This stated that the land, water, and forest resources of minority communities should be under their own control. Although this law is often ignored by nontribal peoples, it has been partially effective in giving minority peoples greater confidence about their rights to use their lands and forests in a sustainable way.

Living in Towns and Cities

Today more than one in four Indians live in a town or city. The four largest cities are the country's capital, New Delhi; Mumbai (Bombay), capital of the western state of Maharashtra; Kolkata (Calcutta), capital of the eastern state of West Bengal; and Chennai (Madras), capital of the southern state of Tamil Nadu (TAH-meel NAH-doo). Mumbai is the largest city, with a population estimated at nearly thirteen million. At least twenty other cities have populations of more than one million, including Ahmedabad (AH-muh-duh-bahd), Bangalore, and Hyderabad.

The cities of India are among the fastest growing and most densely populated in the world. This is partly because India's population is expanding so rapidly, but also because of migration from the rural areas; people are flooding into the cities in search of work. The infrastructure simply cannot keep up; there is a shortage of housing, transport, water, and sanitation. Most cities are overcrowded, their streets packed with traffic, people, and animals. Pollution is an increasing worry to city dwellers. There is serious air pollution, from traffic and from industry, and also pollution from untreated sewage and garbage. In addition, the crime rate is rising, as the gap between rich and poor continues to widen.

Indians often wonder whether their cities are becoming impossible to live in, yet these cities are also full of energy. Life is tough for the majority of India's urban dwellers, yet their survival skills and enterprise somehow shine through. India's cities are hubs of trading, with small businesses and rapidly growing companies and industries. They are also rich in culture and entertainment.

The contrast between the lives of the rich and the poor is most evident in their homes—or lack of them. Many ordinary city dwellers live in crowded apartment buildings, sharing rooms with relatives and basic kitchen and bathroom facilities with the many other tenants. Wealthier families tend to live in separate areas, where houses are stylish and spacious. Walled compounds protect them from the world outside and provide space for well-tended gardens and living quarters for the servants.

The shortage of cheap housing means that millions of India's poor end up in slums or living on the streets. The outskirts of cities overflow with slum areas, full of hastily built shanty homes constructed from scraps of tin, wood, and mud. Many people have no homes at all and may live almost their whole lives on the streets.

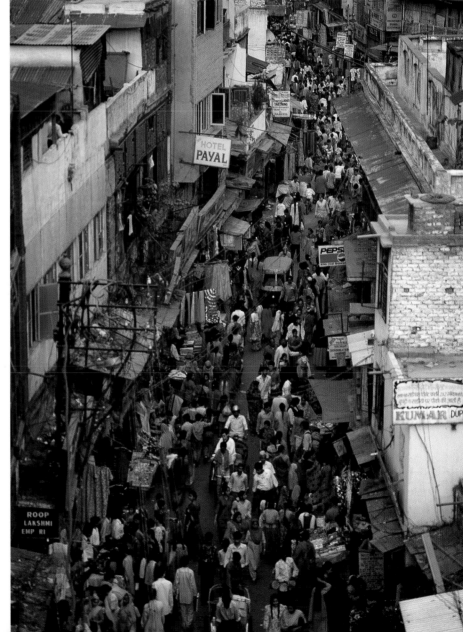

Most Indian cities are overcrowded, their streets packed with traffic, people, and animals. This busy small street is in the Paraganj area of New Delhi.

Kolkata

With a population of over 11 million, Kolkata is one of the largest cities in the world. It is also a major port and industrial center.

Kolkata often seems to personify the best and the worst of India's cities. Many people's image of Kolkata is often of appalling poverty, overcrowding, slums, and workers' strikes. Many of the city's problems arise because it has long absorbed thousands of migrants from poorer Indian states and waves of refugees from Bangladesh.

Yet, under West Bengal's long-established communist government, Kolkata has seen many changes. It has a world-class subway system, software technology parks, and lots of new housing plans. Its Science City is the largest in India. Kolkata is also famous for its lively and creative people: it is home to many leading writers, moviemakers, and musicians.

Pedestrians near a mosque in Kolkata. The city offers many places of worship for India's different religions, including temples, churches, and mosques.

Millions of the poor in India's cities are unemployed or have little work. Yet, as the cities expand, people find work in all sorts of areas: as laborers on building sites; as petty traders selling on the streets; as clothes washers. Some even make a living from scavenging garbage piles.

India's middle class is expanding rapidly, as the demand grows for office workers and business and professional people, such as teachers, doctors, and lawyers. The major cities are also centers of large global companies, run by highly successful international businessmen and women.

Mumbai is India's number one city for industry, finance, and trade. It is also the largest and richest city in India, and it is a magnet for people from all over the country seeking their fortunes. New Delhi, the capital city, is smaller. It became India's capital in the early twentieth century, and the modern architecture of its center combines European and Indian influences with well-laid out streets. In the south, fast-growing Bangalore has developed as India's leading city in modern industry. It has many computer software and hardware companies and telecommunications industries. It boasts leading educational and research institutions and is the base for India's space program.

Living in the Countryside

Most Indians—nearly three-fourths of the population—live in rural areas. Village life centers on farming, the seasons, the family, and the village community. Most rural families are poor by Western standards. They work very hard to make ends meet. Women's work, especially, is constant: cleaning, preparing food, collecting fuel and water, and working in the fields. From an early age, children are expected to help with chores.

There are more than half a million named villages in India. Villages can vary greatly in size: many are small, while others have hundreds of inhabitants. The houses are built close together. Depending on its size, the village may have a temple or religious shrine, a village well or faucet, a pond or tank for irrigation and washing, and a village square. Beyond the village are the farmers' fields and grazing land for livestock, which villagers often share.

Village houses are normally made from local materials, such as bricks, clay, or sandstone. Family homes consist of simple rooms, with little furniture. Most have concrete or earth floors. There is usually a separate kitchen or an outdoor area for cooking, which is kept spotlessly clean, and, in Hindu homes, a shrine to the family's god. There is often a family courtyard, where many daily activities take place, and, depending on region, a pond for bathing and washing clothes and dishes. In the hottest weather people sleep outside in the courtyard or on the roof.

Village Life: Tradition and Change

To an outsider, life in an Indian village may seem simple and unchanging. Yet village life is not simple: people are bound together by complex networks—of caste, extended families, and work—that connect with other villages and with cities. Wealthier villagers are usually from higher-caste families, and they often own the land that poorer families farm. There are also particular occupations that are based on caste and are handed down from

A woman in West Bengal looking after her hens. Some rural families now produce food to sell, as well as for their own needs.

A village square in Rajasthan, northwest India. Village squares often have large shade trees under which villagers meet to chat, attend meetings, or watch traveling performers.

generation to generation, such as those of barber, weaver, and priest. Only dalits, known as the untouchables, are leatherworkers—contact with animal skins, especially cowhide, is unclean work for other Hindus.

Village life is changing in certain ways. More villages now have electricity and running water. There are more large farms today, producing food to sell to city markets and sometimes overseas. Villages also have links to the wider world. Almost every family has relatives who have gone to work in the towns or cities. Although few homes have their own television or telephones, there may be community facilities for satellite television and movies.

Family Life

The family is at the heart of Indian society. The men have a duty to provide for the family, to run the family business, and to look after the finances. The women are responsible for running the home and religious duties.

One of the reasons why many Indian families are large is because they provide security. The larger the family, the more there are to work, feed, and clothe everyone. Children are the center of family life. Boys, in particular, are cherished. Unlike girls, they stay within the family when they marry. Family wealth and traditions are passed down through the sons. Sons are also expected to look after their parents when they grow old.

The authority and position of all family members are clearly defined. The oldest man, often the grandfather, is head of the household. His wife is in charge of the younger women, making sure that all the work gets done.

In most families it is still customary for parents to choose potential husbands or

The Panchayats: India's Village Councils

In ancient India rural communities had a well-organized system of village councils known as panchayats *(pahn-CHIE-uhts). Members of the panchayats were senior men from the higher castes in the village, including a headman. They were the decision makers, who sorted disputes and punished wrongdoers.*

Under the British, panchayats lost much of their authority, but they were revived in several states after independence. Today they cover most of India. Villagers elect panchayat members from within the village. By law, these must now include women and low-caste members. The panchayats have the authority and money to develop their village. This might include improving local roads or the water supply, building a primary health center, or introducing adult literacy programs.

They may no longer share the same house, but often live very near one another. And no matter how long people have lived in a city, they still feel they belong to their family home in the village.

Women and Girls in the Family

Hinduism reveres womanhood, and Hindus worship many powerful goddesses. Yet when a girl child is born into a family, she is often seen as a burden. This is because her family will probably have to pay dowry—often a large sum of money—to her husband's family when she marries. She then leaves her parents' home to live with her husband's family.

In the family home, men have authority over women. Yet some women are beginning to have greater independence, especially over money matters. There are a growing number of women's organizations and thrift cooperatives. These may provide finance to help women set up small businesses or to invest in labor-saving equipment for the home.

Violence against women is not uncommon, especially for lower caste and

wives for their children. Today some couples, usually city dwellers, may opt for a love match rather than an arranged marriage.

Although work and living patterns are changing in India, especially in the cities, the family is still central. When people move to urban areas, they rely on family members to help them find work and a place to live.

A family from Tamil Nadu, southern India. The traditional Indian family often has four generations living in the family home.

Marriage brings together two families, not just the couple, so choosing the right partner—usually from the same caste and background—is extremely important.

dalit women. Some people believe that, as women seek more rights, violence against them has increased.

Food and Drink

There are also rituals and taboos associated with food, often for religious reasons. For Hindus, the cow is sacred and must never be killed, so they do not eat beef. Many follow vegetarian diets. Muslims regard the pig as an unclean animal and must not eat pork. Jains, with their reverence for all living things, are strict vegetarians.

Hindus follow special rituals when preparing food. Most are concerned with purity and cleanliness. According to tradition, a high-caste Hindu cannot eat food prepared by someone from a low caste, because the food will then become impure. Indians wash their hands both before and after eating and will not eat in the morning before bathing. People often eat with their fingers, always using the right hand, or scoop sauces up with pieces of flatbread. In traditional homes, men and women usually eat separately.

Regional Differences

Some foods and ingredients are found throughout India: flatbreads of different kinds, rice, dairy produce, as well as a wide range of vegetables and spices. The long-standing practice of vegetarianism means that Indian cooks have developed many wonderful dishes based on vegetables,

A Few Indian Spices

Indians cook with many different spices, depending on where they live, family traditions, and personal taste. Spices may be used whole, ground, roasted, or blended into a paste. Different combinations of spices are used to draw out a range of flavors in individual dishes.

Some of the most widely used spices are aromatic seeds, such as cardamom, coriander, cumin (KOO-mihn), and mustard seed. Ginger and turmeric, which gives intense yellow color to food, come from rootlike plant stems. Cinnamon, fragrant and sweet, comes from tree bark. Tamarind (TA-muh-rihnd), the pulp from a large seedpod, has a mildly acid taste. The most expensive spice, saffron, is from a crocus flower; it adds a delicate yellow color to rice.

beans, and different spices. Beans provide protein in a nonmeat diet. An everyday dish for many Indians is *dhal* (DAWL), a kind of sauce that can be made from lentils, dried peas, or beans.

In the north, food reflects the influence of the Mogul period in Indian history. Northern farmers grow a lot of wheat, so flatbreads, such as chapatis (chuh-PAH-teez) or naan, accompany most meals. People eat more meat than in southern India. Tandoori dishes are a specialty: meat is first marinated in herbs, spices, and yogurt and then cooked in a clay oven. Some dishes are elaborate blends, reflecting those created for the Mogul courts. Ingredients may include cream or yogurt, dried and fresh fruit, nuts, and spices, such as saffron.

Southern Indians, who are mostly Hindus, eat more vegetarian food. Their

Women in Rajasthan, northwest India, sorting red chilies for drying in the sun. Chilies are small, hot peppers, used fresh or dried to add spiciness to many dishes.

diet also reflects the geography and climate of the region. Many southern farmers grow rice, and rice is eaten with most meals. Rice is also ground, like flour, to make *dosa* (DOE-zah), a type of pancake, and *iddlis* (EED-lihs), steamed savory cakes that are often eaten at breakfast. Seafood and fresh fish are caught along the coast and on the inland waterways. Southern cooking is often hot and spicy, and coconut milk is a popular ingredient in many dishes.

Drinks, Snacks, and Digestives

Tea is widely drank in India, usually heavily sweetened with sugar and milk. Coffee, the favorite drink in the south, is becoming increasingly fashionable. Cool drinks include lassi, made from yogurt. Soft drinks are also very popular. Many Indians do not drink alcohol, but beer and spirits are popular among those who do. In rural areas, local alcoholic brews are often made from honey and fruits.

Lassi

Lassi *(LAH-see) is a cold and refreshing drink that is popular throughout India. You can top it with whatever you like, including chopped fruit, nuts, or flavored syrup.*

You will need:

8 tbsp (120 grams) sugar
3 cups (710 milliliters) yogurt
¾ cup (180 millilites) water
4 tbsp (60 grams) whipping cream

Mix the sugar and yogurt. Add water and blend the mixture in an electric blender until smooth and fluffy. Refrigerate until it becomes ice cold. Serve chilled, topped with whipped cream.

Snacking is popular in India. There are roadside stalls everywhere, selling all kinds of savory snacks as well as fruit, including mangoes, papaya, bananas, pineapples, and coconuts.

After meals, especially after a rich feast, people like to serve digestives to help prevent indigestion and also to cleanse the mouth and sweeten the breath. The digestive is usually a plate of *paan*. Paan is made from *betel* (BEE-tuhl) leaf—a type of creeping plant—rolled into a small triangle and filled with special ingredients, such as

Roadside stall sellers offer all kinds of savory snacks, including fried pastries, known as samosas; *roasted nuts; and* channa *made from spiced chickpeas.*

Indian Desserts

Indian desserts are usually very sweet and rich, more like candy than puddings. Desserts made at home are not normally part of daily meals, but are prepared specially for festivals and celebrations. Many Indians also regularly buy freshly made candies, from small candy stores and street stalls.

Many use milk as the main ingredient. The milk is simmered slowly for several hours until it is thick and concentrated. Gulab jamon (goo-LAB JAH-muhn: cake-like fried milk balls in scented syrup) are made in this way. Kulfi is a delicious Indian ice cream made from concentrated milk, cardamom, and pistachio nuts.

aniseed, cumin, cardamom, spearmint, or liquorice. Some Indians even like to chew paan throughout the day.

Leisure and Sport

The most popular regular leisure activities, for Indians of all ages and backgrounds, are watching television and going to the movies. Leisure activities are often centered around family, and family outings to parks, beaches, ancient temples, and other sights are very popular. More and more Indians are also taking vacations, to see their own land and to visit countries overseas.

The towns and cities offer many different types of entertainment for those who can afford them. There are restaurants, clubs, movie theaters, sports stadiums, and horse-racing tracks. In the villages most people have little time to relax, and there aren't many facilities around. When they do have the time, leisure activities include going to

Playing cards with friends is a popular pastime. Here local tradesmen play cards outside the Jain "Red Temple" in Ajmer, Rajasthan, northwest India.

local fairs and festivals, watching dramas put on by traveling performers, relaxing with friends and family, playing cards, or just chatting.

Favorite team sports today, both to take part in and to watch, are soccer, cricket, and field hockey. Badminton and volleyball are also enjoyed. Enthusiasts play soccer and cricket wherever they can: in backyards, quiet city streets, and open spaces, as well as in sports grounds. More wealthy Indians often join tennis and golf clubs.

The national cricket and field hockey teams compete successfully at the international level and are supported passionately by Indian sports fans.

India also has many traditional sports and games. Wrestling, martial arts, dice games, and board games, including chess,

The Kerala snake boat races. Long canoes with tall sterns shaped like the hood of a cobra and rowed by as many as one hundred men race along the inland waterways.

have been played in India for at least three thousand years. The traditional team sport of *kabbadi* (kuh-BAH-dee) is played in villages throughout India. It probably began as a form of self-defense, and it demands fitness and skill. One team sends a "raider" into the other team's court to touch opposing players. The raider has to do this all in one breath, and to prove this he must keeep saying "kabbadi" without stopping. The opposing team tries to catch

Expert kite makers and enthusiastic kite flyers come from all over the world to compete in the International Kite Festival, held each January in Ahmedabad, Gujarat, in western India.

Kites and Kite Flying

Kite flying is popular all over India, but especially in Gujarat, in western India. Every January, at the end of the winter festival of Makar Sankranti *(MAH-kuhr suhn-KRAN-tee), people of all ages bring their fighter kites for the kite flying contests. The string of each fighter kite is coated with glass powder to give it a cutting edge. Friends and strangers go out into the fields or on the city rooftops to battle through the day, trying to cut down their rivals' kites.*

At nighttime, the kite flying is more peaceful. Beautiful illuminated box kites, known as tukkals *(TOO-koolz), are strung on long lines and released into the night sky.*

and hold the raider. Any player who is touched or caught is out.

Some sports are regional. In Kerala, in the southwest, the snake boat races in August are the highlight of the sporting year. In the semidesert state of Rajasthan, in the northwest, camel races are much loved by festival- and fair-goers.

Literature

Indians have a love of storytelling that goes back thousands of years.

For a long time most of India's literature was oral: tales, epics, and poems were learned by heart and handed down from generation to generation. The most famous stories, which almost every Indian learns as a small child, are the *Mahabharata* and the *Ramayana*. These epic poems date back over two thousand years.

The *Mahabharata* has over one hundred thousand verses and is the longest poem in the world. It contains many different episodes, but it tells mostly of the battles between groups of royal cousins to rule ancient India.

The *Ramayana*, with the story of Prince Rama and his beautiful wife, Sita, at its heart, continues to enchant modern-day Indians. Performances of the different tales draw large and enthusiastic crowds in villages and cities alike. Over the centuries philosopher, is probably the most highly regarded in India.

From the time of Mogul and British rule, Indian poets and novelists began to write extensively in the major Indian languages, as well as in English. In the east, Bengal became a hothouse of writing talent from the nineteenth century onward. The most influential—and most loved—of Bengali writers was Rabindranath Tagore. Tagore was a political, spiritual, and educational leader, but he was also a creative and energetic writer. He produced volumes of poetry, stories, plays, songs, and children's literature. He also founded a university called Santiniketan

A Diwali picture showing Rama (center), his brother, Lakshmana (left), and wife, Sita (right). Hanuman, the monkey king, kneels at the front.

many versions of the *Ramayana* have evolved, told in different Indian languages and with distinct regional variations.

The *Mahabharata* and *Ramayana* were later written down in Sanskrit and other Indian languages. They have also been translated into other languages and made into movies and television sagas.

The arrival of Islam brought new influences to Indian literature. During the time of the Moguls, poetry in Persian and Urdu became fashionable. Islamic literature in Urdu continued to develop under British rule and after independence. The poetry of Mirza Ghalib and later of Muhammad Iqbal, the Muslim leader and

The Tales of the Ramayana

Prince Rama was the son of a wise king in the royal city of Ayodhya. His jealous stepmother forced the king to banish Rama for fourteen years. Rama, his loyal brother Lakshmana, and his wife, Sita, lived as hermits in the forest and faced many adventures.

During their exile a ten-headed demon, Ravana, kidnapped Sita and carried her off to Lanka, his island kingdom. The brothers searched high and low. Finally, with the help of Hanuman, the monkey king, they found Sita. Hanuman and his army of forest animals built a bridge to the island, and after many battles, Rama killed Ravana and rescued Sita.

At last, Rama and Sita returned to their kingdom. The people rejoiced: good had defeated evil and true love had won.

Arundhati Roy, the author of The God of Small Things, *which became an international best-seller. She is also a political campaigner, in particular against the Narmada Valley Dams.*

Music, Dance, and Drama

Many of India's music, dance, and drama traditions have their origins in religion.

Indian classical music has its origins in the chanting of verses from the Vedas, the Hindu sacred texts. From this, the Indian classical tradition has developed in quite a different way from Western music. It is often very complex, but there are two basic elements: the raga, or melody, and the tala, or rhythm. India has many different types of musical instruments, including stringed and wind instruments and drums. The best known are probably the sitar, a large stringed instrument, and the tabla, a pair of drums.

The regions of India have their own styles of folk music. There are innumerable

A band from Karnataka, southern India. Many musicians and singers do not receive training, but pick up the songs and music through community and village occasions.

(SAWN-tih-nee-keh-tahn) that was devoted to the arts. In 1913 he won the Nobel Prize for Literature.

Indian literature continues to flourish, both in Indian languages and in English. With growing literacy in India, writers have been able to reach new audiences. They have also found many readers overseas. In the 1930s Mulk Raj Anand wrote protest novels, giving a voice to the poor, low caste, and untouchables. R. K. Narayan wrote novels and short stories for more than sixty years, creating a whole world through the characters he portrayed in the fictional town of Malgudi. More recently, novelists such as Anita Desai, Arundhati Roy, and Rohinton Mistry, with their sensitive portrayals of life in modern India, have won international literary prizes.

Bharat Natyam dancers from Tamil Nadu in southern India. This is one of the most beautiful styles of classical dance.

learning and perfecting the demanding dance styles.

Manipuri (muh-nih-POOR-ee) dancing, from eastern India, tells how the god Krishna played his flute and danced in the moonlight with the cowgirls who tended their herds nearby. Kathak dancing has its origins in northern India. The graceful foot movements and tinkling ankle bells resemble the dancers painted in Mogul miniatures. The most dramatic form of dance is Kathakali (kuh-thuh-KAH-lee), from Kerala.

songs, instruments, and dances. They are often played at festivals and fairs, at weddings and birth ceremonies, or at planting and harvest time.

Bhangra is the folk music and dance of the Punjab in northern India. Drums, voices, and clapping accompany the dances, which celebrate the harvest festival of Baisakhi (bee-SAH-kee). In the West, Bhangra has also been popularized as dance music, through its mixing with modern Western instruments and rhythms.

The music that most Indians are familiar with today comes from "Bollywood" movies. Like Bhangra, they blend Indian traditions and Western music.

Classical Dance

According to ancient Hindu texts, dancing came from the gods, above all from Shiva, the "lord of the dance." Hindu sculptures often show dancers and the poses, facial expressions, feet and hand movements of different dances. Dances were performed in temples to please the gods and goddesses. Temple dancers often devoted their lives to

Kathakali

Kathakali is a dance drama, traditionally performed only by men. Dancers mime stories from the Ramayana *and* Mahabharata. *A cast of colorful characters appear, gods and goddesses, heroes and villains, saints and demons, and princesses and peasants.*

Kathakali performances start at dusk and may last all night. As the dancers perform, singers tell the story. The dramatic costumes, masklike makeup, and headdresses transform each performer and are an essential part of Kathakali. The color of the makeup indicates the character: the hero's face is green, demons are red, and women — usually played by boys — are yellow.

The postures and different hand and feet movements in Kathakali are extremely demanding. Performers must be very fit; training takes at least six years and is based on traditional Keralan martial arts.

Folk Dance Dramas

Folk dance dramas are very popular, and different regions have their own styles and traditions. They may use puppets, masks, or stilts and are often performed during festivals. Some are linked with the seasons. Traveling performers also put on dance dramas for village communities, retelling the adventures of the Hindu gods.

In recent times Indian dancers and choreographers have experimented with both classical Indian and Western influences to develop new styles of dance. Perhaps the best known of these modern dancers is Chandralekha (chun-druh-LEH-kuh), who has used dance, yoga, film, and political issues in her interpretations of modern Indian dance.

Movies

India has the largest movie industry in the world. In an average year around eight hundred movies are made—about eight times more than in the United States. India's movie industry is so successful that it is also one of the fastest growing global industries.

India has a long history of filmmaking. The first Indian movies were made nearly one hundred years ago. In the first half of the twentieth century, the subjects often dealt with serious issues, such as nationalism and uniting India's different peoples and religions. In the 1950s the Bengali director and writer Satyajit Ray began making his first films. Of these, the Apu trilogy is now regarded as a classic of world movies. It tells the story of Apu, his village childhood, his family's poverty, and his move to school and college in the big city.

Today the heart of Indian filmmaking is Mumbai, but movies are also made in other cities, such as Kolkata and Chennai. The movie industry in Mumbai is often called

A movie-house billboard in New Delhi shows the glamour, romance, and adventure that Indian moviegoers expect in a typical Bollywood film.

The Bahai Temple (or Lotus Temple), Delhi. This breathtaking temple is open to all faiths. The lotus is the national flower of India, signifying purity and peace.

Bollywood. The movies are made in Hindi, but the songs are usually sung in Urdu.

Bollywood movies appeal to all levels and all ages in Indian society. Most are stories of love and adventure, with plenty of songs, dances, exotic settings, and gorgeous costumes along the way. For villagers and poor urban dwellers, they offer an escape into a life of glamour, romance, and adventure.

Indian movies are also famous for their stars, who are hero-worshiped by their fans. Probably the most legendary star today is Amitabh Bachchan, who has millions of adoring fans. He has starred in more than one hundred movies, and in 2001 he was awarded the Star of the Century award at the Alexandria International Film Festival in Egypt.

Art and Architecture

The traditions of Indian art and architecture can be traced back over nearly four thousand years. Inspiration for many of the greatest works — the sculptures, carvings, paintings, and temples — has almost always come from religion, at first the great Indian religions of Hinduism, Jainism, and Buddhism, and later from Islam. Over the centuries different traditions have influenced and often overlapped with each other.

Buddhist art and architecture flowered from the third century B.C.E. until the thirteenth century C.E. Buddhist craftsmen were skilled in working with stone. They built temples and monasteries, often carved from rock caves. They created stupas — stone structures built to remember the Buddha's life and teachings — and carved pillars. They sculpted huge, beautiful images of the Buddha. In the caves of Ajanta in Maharashtra State, western India, are some of the finest surviving examples of Buddhist art.

The Jains have built temples, often on hilltops, where their saints are believed to have preached. The Shatrunjaya Hill, near

The Taj Mahal, in Agra, Uttar Pradesh, northern India, shows the fine symmetry of Islamic architecture. The gardens are designed to reflect paradise.

The Taj Mahal

The Taj Mahal is often described as the most beautiful building in the world. It was built in the seventeenth century as a garden tomb for Mumtaz, the beloved wife of the Mogul Emperor, Shah Jahan.

Islamic architecture uses symmetry to achieve harmony and beauty, and the Taj Mahal is a perfect example of this. From white marble domes and tapering minarets to gardens and water channels, all are in perfect balance.

The Taj Mahal appears to change color at different times of day. Its white marble has a pinkish hue at dawn and is milky white in the evening. At full moon, visitors flock to see its color turn to gold.

Palitana, Gujarat, is home to 863 beautifully carved Jain temples. The most beautiful examples of Jain architecture are the exquisitely carved white marble temples at Mount Abu in Rajasthan.

The Hindus have built temples throughout India, from the smallest village shrines to large temple complexes. Over the centuries, the carving and decoration of these temples became more and more ornate and colorful. Sculptures and paintings brought Hindu gods and goddesses to life in fantastic scenes from the great epics, the *Mahabharata* and the *Ramayana*.

The Islamic influence in India is seen most clearly through its architecture, above all from the time of the great Mogul rulers. They became famous for the building of forts, tombs, and mosques, found mostly in northern India. Mogul artists designed fine gardens and crafted decorated tiles and inlaid marble. The Moguls also introduced the Persian tradition of miniature painting. Persian artists at the Mogul courts trained local artists in this new technique. The Persian style is also reflected in Hindu Rajput paintings. Mogul miniatures mostly showed court life, while the Rajput paintings illustrated tales from the Hindu epics. There are Indian artists today who continue to paint in this detailed, richly colored style.

Western styles began to influence Indian art and architecture during the period of British rule. Since independence, Indian artists have sought inspiration from a range of sources, including modern Western influences as well as Indian religious, regional, and folk traditions. In architecture, Chandigarh (CHUN-dih-goor) in northwest India was planned as a complete, modern city by the French architect Le Corbusier and local Indian architects.

Everyday Decorative Arts and Crafts

Although many goods are now mass-produced, craft traditions in India remain strong. Skilled craftspeople from all parts of the country continue to make many different items that are both practical and beautiful. Craft skills are handed down from generation to generation, particularly in the villages.

Working with textiles has always been an important local industry. Textile work includes spinning, weaving, batik (a method of hand-printing a fabric by covering the parts that will not be dyed with removable wax), and embroidery of clothing and household items. Saris (SAH-rees), skirts, and blouses may have exquisite embroidery details, such as threads of real gold or silver or tiny mirrors, which are especially popular in Rajasthan and Gujarat. Woolen and silk shawls are more common in some of the northern states, such as Punjab and Kashmir, where it can get very cold in winter. Kashmir is also famous for carpet weaving.

There is an enormous demand for jewelry—India probably imports more gold than any other country in the world. Jewelry makers may blend modern and traditional designs, according to fashion, working with gold and silver, precious and semi-precious gems.

There is also a huge market for practical, decorative items for the home, including pottery, brass and silverware, baskets, metal, wood furniture, and rugs.

Decorative art comes into its own on special occasions, such as festivals and weddings. The women in the household decorate the home: the floors, walls, doorways, and courtyard. They may use colored powders or rice flour to create complicated patterns or pictures called

Lengths of sari material. The sari is a long piece of cloth worn by many Indian women. It is draped in different ways according to caste, age, region, and religion.

This girl is having her palms decorated with the beautiful patterns of mehendi. *The patterns fade gradually and may last for several weeks.*

alpona or *rangoli*. One of the most popular decorative arts is *mehendi* (muh-HAEN-dee), which has become an important ritual in wedding preparations. The day before the wedding, female relatives decorate the bride's hands and feet with mehendi, a paste made from henna. After washing, the intricate patterns turn rusty red, a color said to bring good luck. The name of the groom is often hidden in the patterns.

A modern form of uniquely Indian decorative art can be seen in the posters, billboards, and signs that advertise all sorts of things, from the latest movies or soft drinks to political parties and small businesses.

Religion

Religion has shaped almost every aspect of life in India: its history, art and architecture, literature, music and dance, festivals, dress, and food. Two of the world's major religions, Hinduism and Buddhism, began in India. Jainism and Sikhism also began here.

Today about 80 percent of the population is Hindu, and more than 10 percent is Muslim. Other religions with significant followings include Christianity, Sikhism, Buddhism, and Jainism. There are also Jews, followers of tribal religions, and much smaller communities of Parsis, who follow the Zoroastrian (soe-roe-AS-tree-uhn) faith that originated in Persia.

Hinduism

Hinduism is the oldest of the world's great religions. It probably developed from the mixing of Dravidian and Aryan beliefs more than three thousand years ago. Hinduism has no founder or prophet, but its beliefs and practices have been shaped over many hundreds of years. As Hinduism developed it became a complete way of life. Today it is the third largest of the major world religions.

Over the centuries, other important Indian religions have developed from Hinduism. Unlike Hinduism, these religions had founders—religious thinkers who began to question some of Hinduism's rigid beliefs and practices. They include Jainism and Buddhism, both dating from the sixth century B.C.E., and Sikhism, which began in the sixteenth century C.E.

The Core Beliefs of Hinduism

Hindus believe that there is one universal spirit, Brahman (BRAH-muhn), which exists everywhere and in everything. It has no form and is neither male nor female. The spirit of Brahman is so powerful it cannot be understood by human beings.

Hindus believe in a cycle of birth, life, death, and rebirth, which they call samsara. When a person dies, his or her soul does not die, but moves on to another living being. Every Hindu hopes they will eventually break free of the cycle of samsara. When the soul is completely pure, it will return to where it began, to become a tiny part of Brahman. Hindus also believe in karma. Karma refers to the consequences of action, and it determines what happens when a person's soul is reborn. If a person lives his present life badly, he will take a step down in his next life because of his bad karma. He may be reborn as an animal, not as a human. A person who lives their life well will take a step up and gradually move closer to Brahman.

Hinduism also teaches that there is a natural law that governs every aspect of a person's life. This is known as dharma.

The Caste System

Hindus' belief in the law of dharma is reflected in the caste system. This states that everyone belongs to a particular group in society and does a particular job within that group. An individual is born into that group or caste, and so are his or her children, grandchildren, and all their future descendants. People cannot change the caste into which they were born, nor the type of work they do.

There are four main groups in the caste system and many subgroups within each of these. The highest group is the Brahmins, the priest class. The second group is the Kshastriyas (SHAS-tree-yahz), the warriors and rulers. Vaishyas (VEESH-yuhs), the farmers and traders, make up the third group, while Shudras, the unskilled workers and peasants, are the lowest caste. Outside the caste system are the dalits, or untouchables.

Hindu priests have to remain pure because they touch religious objects in the temples. For this reason they are almost always Brahmins. They cannot eat any food prepared by a person from a lower caste. The untouchables, regarded as unclean, have always done the worst and dirtiest jobs. In the past they had to keep themselves apart from higher castes. They were not allowed to go to school or to visit temples. In the twentieth century, laws were passed to give rights to untouchables. They often call themselves *dalits*, meaning "oppressed" or "downtrodden."

A Brahmin priest performs puja (ceremony or worship) at a family home. High-caste Hindus may invite a priest to lead the rituals at important life-cycle ceremonies.

Sadhus: Wandering Holy Men

Sadhus (*SAH-dooz*) are holy men who give up their families, homes, and all their possessions to follow their religious convictions. They spend their lives traveling alone, carrying little money or food. Other Hindus give them food in return for their blessing and religious wisdom.

In order to gain religious understanding and become closer to Brahman, many sadhus undertake frequent periods of fasting or may sit or stand completely still for a long time. Some withdraw alone to remote places to spend their lives in meditation and prayer. Most sadhus have a personal guru, a religious teacher, who they visit from time to time.

Many sadhus never cut their hair or beards. They often smear their bodies with ashes from holy fires. There are an estimated four to five million sadhus in India today.

In the cities the caste system is less important today. People from different castes work together, meet socially, and sometimes marry. In most Indian villages the caste system continues to play an important part in everyday life and work.

Gods and Goddesses

Hinduism has thousands of minor gods and goddesses. Hindus believe that each one shows just one small part of Brahman and can help humans begin to understand the meaning of Brahman. Above all these minor deities are three gods who show the main forms of Brahman. They are Brahma (the creator), Vishnu (the preserver), and Shiva (the destroyer). Vishnu sometimes comes down to Earth in the form of minor deities, known as avatars (AH-vuh-tahrz). Some avatars of Vishnu include Krishna and Rama. Krishna is one of the most popular Hindu gods, often seen as the god of love, and in the *Mahabharata* epic he experiences many adventures. Rama is often portrayed as the ideal man for his courage and loyalty and is the hero of the *Ramayana*. Hanuman, the monkey god, is Rama's faithful helper. Goddesses include Lakshmi, the wife of Vishnu and goddess of wealth, and Parvati, the wife of Shiva. Ganesh, the elephant-headed god, is the son of Shiva and Parvati, and he is believed to bring good luck.

Worship

Most Hindu worship, known as *puja*, takes place in the family home. Every home has a small shrine with an image—a picture or statue—of the family's special god. Hindus

Women stand in line outside a Hindu temple in Kolkata. They carry small gifts, including flowers, to offer the temple gods. Before entering the temple, they always remove their shoes.

do not worship the image itself, but it serves to bring them closer to Brahman. The family shrine is lovingly cared for. Flowers, incense, and lights are placed before the image, and symbolic offerings of food and water are made. At home, Hindus pray every day, often repeating verses from the holy books or silently meditating. The women in the family take responsibility for looking after the shrine and also for teaching the children Hindu traditions and rituals.

Hindus may also worship at their local temple. A temple is often constructed where a god or goddess is believed to have lived or appeared on Earth. It may be tiny, large, or even part of a huge temple complex. Every temple has a shrine to the god or goddess, which only a Hindu priest can care for. Hindus may worship at any time, and there is no group worship.

Pilgrimage

Traveling on pilgrimage to holy places is an important part of Hinduism. Hindus believe that bathing in a holy river helps to wash away sins and become closer to Brahman. The greatest of India's holy

The Ganga River at Varanasi, Uttar Pradesh, northern India. Several towns on the Ganga are important to Hindu pilgrims, but Varanasi is considered the holiest of all.

rivers is the Ganga; millions travel to bathe in its waters or arrange to have their ashes scattered on its waters after they die. There are many other sacred places throughout India, where Hindus believe that a god once appeared or a miracle happened. There are many mountain shrines high in the Himalayas, home of the gods and where the source of the holy Ganga rises.

Hindu Festivals

Hindus share a wealth of festivals; they occur throughout the year and in all parts of India. Many are local festivals, found only in a particular region. Most are religious and follow the lunar calendar, the monthly cycle of the moon, so they fall on different days each year. They also celebrate Western holidays, such as Christmas and New Year.

Diwali (dih-WAH-lee) is one of the most popular Hindu festivals. It is the festival of lights, when people fill their homes with candles and lamps. The lights symbolize

A street lit up for Diwali. During this festival almost every town and village in India is magically lit with thousands of flickering candles, lamps, and lights.

goodness and understanding, driving away evil and ignorance. People remember how the brave Prince Rama finally triumphed over evil in the Hindu epic the *Ramayana*.

Diwali falls at the end of the rainy season, in October or November, when farmers bring in the harvest. For businesspeople, it is the end of the financial year, a time to put their accounts in order. People also look forward to a successful year ahead. Lakshmi, the goddess of wealth, is especially important at this time. Pictures and statues of Lakshmi are garlanded with flowers and given offerings of food.

Diwali is celebrated in different ways in different parts of India. It may last from three to five days. Families and friends exchange cards and presents, visit each other's homes, and share special foods.

Navaratri (nuh-vuh-RAH-tree), the festival of "nine nights," usually falls in October and is very popular throughout India. It celebrates the mother goddess in her different forms. In Bengal she is honored as Durga, the fearless warrior who defeated the buffalo demon. Dussehra (DOOSH-rah) follows on the tenth day and

Kumbh Mela

Hindu legend tells how gods and demons once fought to extract divine nectar from the ocean. As the kumbh *(KOOM: pot) of nectar was being carried to heaven, several drops fell to Earth and landed in twelve places. One was the meeting point of the Ganga and Yamuna Rivers, near Allahabad in northern India. Hindus believe this confluence of holy rivers has special powers to cleanse the soul.*

The Kumbh Mela takes place here every twelve years. It is open to people of all faiths, to take part in prayers and share religious knowledge. For Hindu pilgrims, bathing in the holy waters is the most important part of Kumbh Mela.

A procession during Kumbh Mela, in Uttar Pradesh, in 2001. An estimated thirty million pilgrims took part, the largest gathering of people anywhere on Earth.

is dedicated to Prince Rama. In many parts of India, but especially in Gujarat, people act out stories from the *Ramayana* and burn huge effigies to celebrate Rama's victory over the demon Ravana.

Holi is the most high-spirited of the Hindu festivals, marking the beginning of spring in February or March. Its name comes from the wicked demon, Holika, and on the night before the festival, bonfires are lit to symbolize her destruction. Holi is also associated with the mischievous god Krishna. On the day of Holi, people play tricks—just as Krishna loved to do. They hold water fights and throw colored water or powders over one another.

Jainism

Jainism began about 2,500 years ago, although its origins are believed to go back much farther. Today there are estimated to be between four and five million Jains in India. Jain tradition says that twenty-four saints, who followed on from one another, began the faith. The last of these saints was Mahavira, who gave up all his wealth and property to seek the meaning of existence. Mahavira taught the importance of a simple, pure, and compassionate life to achieve enlightenment.

Jains follow Mahavira's principles to this day. They believe above all in non-violence, and they will not harm any living thing. Jains are strict vegetarians. Devout Jains, particularly nuns and monks, will eat no root vegetables, or red food because it is the color of blood. Some even wear masks over their mouths and sweep the ground

217

before them to avoid accidentally killing any insect. Like Hindus, Jains believe in karma and in the cycle of birth, life, death, and rebirth.

Jain worship and rituals have much in common with Hinduism. Worship at home or in the temple is performed before images of the Jain saints and the gods that protect them. These images are lovingly cared for and given offerings of food, water, flowers, and incense.

Jains will not work in any profession that has links with acts of violence or killing living things. Many are highly successful in industry, finance, and trade. Jains place great importance on good works, often funding the building of temples, schools, and homes for sick animals. Although Jains only make up a small percentage of India's population, their principles of nonviolence and their business skills have given them a position of influence in Indian society.

This ceremony in Karnataka State follows a tradition started in 981 C.E. Lord Bahubali's statue is bathed in milk, butter, honey, sugar, and water.

Jain Festivals

The main Jain festival is Mahavir Jayanti (MAH-huh-veer jie-AHN-tee), which celebrates the birth of Mahavira. Jain temples are the focus of the celebrations, with special prayers and offerings. Many Jains fast on this day, while others go on a pilgrimage to Jain shrines.

Buddhism

Buddhism also began about 2,500 years ago. Its founder, Siddhartha Gautama, belonged to a royal family from northeast India. He gave up his wealth and spent many years as a wandering holy man, seeking the meaning of life and humanity's suffering. Then one day, after meditating for many, many hours, he believed that he understood why there is suffering in the world. Buddhists call this moment of understanding *enlightenment*. From then Gautama became known as Buddha, the Enlightened One, and spent the rest of his

Exiled Tibetan Buddhist monks play horn music. They wear saffron-colored robes to show their devotion to Buddha. The color saffron symbolizes giving up worldly things.

life traveling, to teach people what he had learned.

Buddhism began in India and spread throughout South and Southeast Asia to become a major world religion. Yet, for several hundred years, it almost disappeared from India. In the twentieth century, numbers increased, with conversions among lower-caste Hindus and with the arrival of refugees from Buddhist Tibet (see CHINA). Today there are estimated to be between five and six million Buddhists in India.

Like Hindus and Jains, Buddhists believe in karma and in the cycle of birth, life, death, and rebirth. However, they do not believe in one all-powerful spirit or God, but focus instead on humankind. The Buddha taught that all humankind finds life imperfect. These feelings of imperfection come from the desire for more material things, from unhappiness within families and within society, and from fear of change and death. Buddhists believe that by following the teaching of the Buddha, a person can begin to overcome these feelings of imperfection, lead a better

life, and perhaps finally reach enlightenment—as the Buddha did.

At the heart of Buddhist worship is meditation. During meditation the worshiper seeks to empty his or her mind of all thoughts and to focus on things above and beyond the stresses and imperfections of everyday life. Meditation helps to calm and control the mind. Meditation may take place at home or in the shrine room of a temple or monastery, where a Buddhist monk or nun guides the worship. Each shrine room has a statue of the Buddha, to which worshipers often make offerings of incense, lighted candles, or flowers.

Buddhist Festivals

Buddhist festivals usually celebrate some aspect of the Buddha's life and teachings. In India the most important of these festivals is known as Buddha Purnima and takes place at full moon, usually in May. Buddhists believe that the Buddha's birth, enlightenment, and death all took place on the same day in different years, and it is on this day that they celebrate Buddha Purnima.

Many Buddhists spend the day worshiping at their local temple or monastery. They bring food for the monks or nuns and listen to readings and talks about the Buddha's life. There are great celebrations in two holy Buddhist cities in

Tens of thousands of pilgrims flock to Bodh Gaya each year to celebrate Buddha Purnima, the most important of Buddhist festivals.

northeastern India: at Bodh Gaya (BOED GIE-uh), where the Buddha achieved enlightenment, and at Sarnath, where he preached to his followers.

Christianity

Christianity first arrived in India nearly two thousand years ago. Indian Christians believe that in 52 C.E. Saint Thomas, one of Jesus' apostles, landed on the coast of Kerala, where he established a small Christian community. Today the number of Christians in India is estimated at more than eighteen million. Most Christians still live on the west coast, in Kerala and Goa. In the last century, missionaries also found

willing converts among minority peoples and low-caste Hindus.

Indian Christians belong to most Protestant denominations, but the majority are Roman Catholics. They celebrate the main Christian festivals of Easter and Christmas. Christmas festivities blend both Western and Hindu traditions: families decorate their homes with lights and paper stars, exchange cards and presents, and prepare special food. Worshipers also decorate churches with scenes from the nativity and attend religious services.

Islam

Islam first arrived in India nearly thirteen hundred years ago, but it only became established as a major Indian religion in the thirteenth century, after Muslim rulers had taken control of the region. Islam has had a strong influence on Indian culture, above all through language, food, art, and architecture. In turn, it has absorbed aspects of Hinduism; many of its festivals and religious practices reflect Hindu influences.

Muslims believe in one God, who they call Allah. He created everything and is beyond all human understanding. They also believe that there were many prophets, including Abraham, Moses, Jesus, and Muhammad. Muhammad was the last of the prophets, the one to whom the Angel Gabriel revealed the word of Allah. These revelations are in the Muslim holy books, above all the Koran, or Qur'an (koo-RAHN), which guides the faithful on all questions of faith and how to live their everyday lives. Muslims are taught to submit completely to the will of Allah and to follow the Five Pillars, or duties, of Islam.

The Five Pillars of Islam are: faith, prayer, almsgiving (giving to the poor), fasting, and pilgrimage. The most important of these is the declaration of faith. Every time Muslims pray, they say the words: "There is no God but Allah, and Muhammad is his prophet." Muslims must pray five times a day, facing Mecca, the Arabian city where Muhammad was born. In Islam, giving alms is a spiritual act, a way of sharing the world's wealth with the poor. Fasting takes place during the month of Ramadan (the ninth month of the Muslim calendar). During this time Muslims must not eat or drink between dawn and sunset. All Muslims hope to make the pilgrimage to the holy city of Mecca at least once in their lives.

Muslims can pray anywhere, at home, at work, or in a mosque. The mosque is the heart of a Muslim community. On Fridays all male Muslims must go to the mosque for midday prayers. Women may go, but they pray separately. There are many beautiful mosques in India, with their distinctive domes and minarets, the towers from which the faithful are called to prayer. The interiors are often decorated with exquisite patterns and geometric shapes; Islam forbids the illustration of any living creature created by Allah.

Sufism, a more mystical form of the faith, has played an important role in the growth of Islam in India. Sufis have often won converts by using local traditions and religious practices in their teachings, including music, dance, and folk stories. More strict Muslims have often disapproved of Sufi practices for being non-Islamic, in particular the worship of saints.

Many of the tombs of long-dead *pir* (PEER), the

Sufi saints, have become important shrines. They are found throughout India and attract Muslim pilgrims from all parts of the country. Some Muslims believe these shrines have special powers—to heal the sick or to address petitions for help directly to Allah.

Muslim Festivals

The two main festivals celebrated by Muslims in India, and throughout the Islamic world, are Eid ul-Fitr (EED uhl-FEET-ruh) and Eid ul-Adha. These festivals fall at different times each year, because the Islamic calendar is a lunar one. Each of the twelve months of the year begins when the new moon rises.

Ramadan takes place during the ninth month of the Islamic year. Muslims believe that it was during this month that Muhammad began to receive the first words of Allah. During Ramadan, Muslims try to lead pure lives, helping one

Muslims at midday prayers at the Jami Masjid mosque in Delhi. The largest mosque in India, it was built during the reign of the seventeenth-century Mogul Emperor, Shah Jahan.

Today about one in ten Indians belongs to the Islamic faith. India has one of the largest Muslim populations in the world.

to the saint's shrine. The celebrations often last for several days. Pilgrims bring petitions and gifts, take part in acts of religious devotion, and share special food prepared in large communal kitchens.

Sikhism

The Sikh religion began in northern India in the sixteenth century. The majority of Sikhs live in the state of Punjab, but there are also substantial communities in other parts of India and throughout the world. With around twenty million followers, Sikhism is recognized as a world religion.

another and submitting to the discipline of fasting. Eid ul-Fitr begins at the end of the month, when the new moon appears. For Muslims it is the most joyful festival. They go to the mosque to give thanks to Allah and give alms to the poor. They wear their best clothes, visit family and friends, exchange cards and presents, and prepare special meals.

Eid ul-Adha coincides with the time of pilgrimage to Mecca. At this time Muslims recall that the prophet Abraham agreed to sacrifice his own son to Allah. Allah spared the boy, and a ram was sacrificed in his place. Muslims mark this festival with prayers and feasting. A ram, or other animal, is killed in the name of Allah. Some of the meat is eaten within the family; the rest is given to the poor.

Indian Muslims also celebrate festivals associated with particular Sufi saints. Every year, on the anniversary of the saint's death, many thousands of Muslims travel

The Five Ks: Symbols of Sikhism

Full members of the Sikh faith wear the five Ks as symbols of their devotion to Sikhism. The first is kesh, *or uncut hair. The Gurus (spiritual leaders) said that Sikhs should never cut their hair, but should keep it clean and tidy. The* kangha *is a comb used to pin the hair in place. Sikh men, and some Sikh women, cover their hair with a turban. The* kara *is a steel bracelet. The circle of the bracelet is a reminder of the eternal nature of God, and the steel symbolizes strength and unity in Sikhism. The* kirpan *is a sword, once used for fighting. Today it is a symbol of spiritual struggle against evil and must never be used to attack.* Kachera *are short pants worn as underwear. First worn by Sikh warriors in battle, today they symbolize modesty and discipline.*

The Golden Temple at Amritsar, Punjab, in northwest India, is the holiest place in the Sikh religion. It is also the most important Sikh gurdwara, or place of worship.

Sikhs follow the teachings of the ten gurus, or spiritual leaders. The founder and first guru was Guru Nanak, who developed the core beliefs of the Sikh religion. Later gurus and their followers were persecuted by India's Muslim rulers for their beliefs, and this led to the founding of a militant brotherhood known as the Khalsa by the tenth and last guru, Guru Gobind Singh. He told Sikhs that after him there would be no more human gurus. Instead they would be guided by their holy book, the Guru Granth Sahib.

Sikhs believe in one all-powerful, eternal God. They believe that everyone is equal before God and reject the Hindu caste system. Like Hindus, they believe in the cycle of birth, life, death, and rebirth. Sikhs believe that by leading a good life and becoming close to God the soul will finally break free of this cycle and be reunited with God forever.

Sikh Festivals

Sikhs have two main types of festivals: *gurpurbs* (GOOR-poorbz), which honor the gurus, and *melas*, or fairs. Sikhs throughout the world celebrate three special gurpurbs, recalling the births of the first and last gurus and the martyrdom of the fifth guru. The Guru Granth Sahib is recited from beginning to end, and it is often carried through the streets with great reverence.

The melas include Baisakhi and Diwali. These are also Hindu festivals, but have special meaning for Sikhs. Baisakhi recalls Guru Gobind Singh and the founding of the Khalsa. Sikhs go to the *gurdwara* (place of worship) to take part in religious celebrations and share a special meal. Diwali is a family festival, when candles and lamps are lit and presents exchanged. Sikhs also remember the persecution of the sixth guru, Guru Hargobind, and the lighting of lamps celebrates his release from prison.

Glossary

Akbar-Nama the illustrated manuscript commissioned by Akbar to record the history of his dynasty. It glorified in colorful paintings the major events of his reign, including successful hunts, victorious battles, and other accomplishments and adventures.

alliance a group of two or more people, organizations, or countries working together with the same aims.

archaeology the scientific study of ancient cultures through the examination of their material remains, such as fossil relics, monuments, and tools.

cash crops a crop grown for direct sale rather than personal use.

caste system the Hindu system of organizing society into classes.

choreography the art of arranging dance movements or routines to music.

civil rights the nonpolitical rights that all citizens have to be treated equally and fairly within a society.

civil war a war between opposing groups of citizens of the same country or nation.

constitution a written statement outlining the laws of a country, stating people's rights and duties and establishing the powers and duties of the government.

dynasty a succession of rulers, all from the same family.

extended family the family as a unit, including children, parents, aunts, uncles, cousins, grandparents, and sometimes more distant relatives.

famine a severe shortage of food, usually resulting in widespread hunger.

fossil fuel a fuel such as coal, oil, or natural gas that is formed in the earth from plant or animal remains.

hostility a feeling of hatred or anger toward somebody.

hydroelectric of or relating to production of electricity from waterpower. The force of a waterfall or dammed river may be used to produce electricity in a power station.

immunization treatment (as with a vaccine) to produce immunity to a disease.

infrastructure the underlying foundation or framework of a company, organization, or other body.

inscription something that is written, engraved, or printed as a lasting record.

insecticide a chemical used to kill insects.

irrigate to supply land with water brought through pipes or ditches.

leprosy an infectious disease that attacks the skin and nerves and can cause deformities and loss of sensation, weight, and strength.

lithograph a print made through a method of printing from a flat surface, such as a stone or metal plate, that has been prepared in such a way that only the areas meant to print will take ink.

maharajah an Indian prince higher in rank than a raja, who is also an Indian prince.

marinate to steep in a sauce or vinegar.

Mesopotamia an ancient region located between the Tigris and Euphrates Rivers in modern Iraq and Syria.

Middle East the countries of southwest Asia and northeast Africa—usually thought to include the countries extending from Libya in the west to Afghanistan in the east.

missionary somebody sent to another country by a church to spread its faith or to do social and medical work.

monopoly complete control over the entire supply of goods or a service in a certain market.

mutiny a refusal to obey authority, especially by soldiers or sailors.

nationalism a loyalty or devotion to one country, especially to a country under foreign control or people.

peninsula a piece of land sticking out from the mainland into a sea or lake.

pilgrim a person who travels to a shrine or holy place to worship.

religious conviction a religious belief or opinion that is held firmly.

revolt to rise up against the authority of a ruler or government.

ritual a traditional ceremony.

Sanskrit an ancient language of India and of Hinduism.

sari a traditional garment worn by women in or from the Indian subcontinent that consists of a long cloth draped around the body and head or shoulder.

separatist a person who favors separation from a religious group, country, or an organization or group of any sort.

slum a poor, run-down, and overcrowded area of a city or town in which the housing is typically in bad condition.

software technology parks special industrial zones with modern, high-tech buildings. They have been set up in many parts of India to encourage Indian software companies to develop and export new software.

taboo forbidden to be used or mentioned because of social or cultural prohibitions.

tuberculosis an infectious disease caused by a bacterium and usually marked by weight loss, fever, coughing, and difficulty in breathing.

untouchable a member of the lowest social caste in India.

uprising an act of rebellion against an authority.

World War I a conflict that broke out in Europe in 1914. The Entente powers, or Allies, (which included the United Kingdom, France, and Russia) fought the Central Powers (which included Austria-Hungary, Germany, and Turkey). The United States joined the Allies in 1917. The war ended in 1918.

World War II a war that began in Europe in 1939 and spread to involve many other countries worldwide. It ended in 1945. The United Kingdom, France, the Soviet Union, the United States, Canada, Australia, New Zealand, and other European countries fought against Germany, Italy, and Japan.

Further Reading

Internet Sites

Look under Countries A to Z in the Atlapedia Online Web Site at
        http://www.atlapedia.com
Use the drop-down menu to select a country on the CIA World Factbook Web Site at
        http://www.odci.gov/cia/publications/factbook
Browse the Table of Contents in the Library of Congress Country Studies Web Site at
        http://lcweb2.loc.gov/frd/cs/cshome.html
Use the Country Locator Maps in the World Atlas Web Site at
        http://www.worldatlas.com/aatlas/world.htm
Look under the alphabetical country listing using the Infoplease Atlas at
        http://www.infoplease.com/countries.html
Use the drop-down menu to select a country using E-Conflict™ World Encyclopedia at
        http://www.emulateme.com
Look under the alphabetical country listing in the Yahooligans Around the World Directory at
        http://www.yahooligans.com/Around_the_World/Countries
Choose the part of the world you're interested in, then scroll down to choose the country using the
Geographia Web Site at
        http://www.geographia.com

India

Ali, Daud. *Step into Ancient India.* New York: Lorenz Books, 2001.
Caldwell, John. *India (Major World Nations).* Philadelphia, PA: Chelsea House Publishers, 1998.
Chatterjee, Manini, and Anita Roy. *Eyewitness: India.* New York: DK Publishing Merchandise, 2002.
Conboy, Fiona, and Sunandini Arora Lal. *Welcome to India (Welcome to My Country).* Milwaukee, WI:
        Gareth Stevens, 2000.
Dalal, Anita. *India (Nations of the World).* Austin, TX: Raintree Steck-Vaughn, 2002.
Einfeld, Jann. *India (History of Nations).* San Diego, CA: Greenhaven Press, 2003.
Engfer, Lee. *India in Pictures.* Minneapolis, MN: Lerner Publications Company, 2002.
Ganeri, Anita. *Exploration into India.* Philadelphia, PA: Chelsea House Publishers, 2000.
Hill, Valerie, and Judith Simpson. *India (Ask about Asia).* Broomall, PA: Mason Crest Publishers, 2003.
Kalman, Bobbie. *India: The People (Land, Peoples, and Cultures).* New York: Crabtree Publishing, 2000.
Lal, Sunandini Arora. *India (Countries of the World).* Milwaukee, WI: Gareth Stevens, 1999.
Lamba, Abha Narain. *Eyewitness Travel Guides: India.* New York: DK Publishing Merchandise, 2002.
Landau, Elaine. *India (True Books).* New York: Children's Press, 1999.
Mamdani, Shelby. *Traditions from India (Cultural Journeys).* Austin, TX: Raintree Steck-Vaughn, 1999.
McCulloch, Julie. *India (World of Recipes).* Chicago, IL: Heinemann Library, 2001.
Murphy, Patricia J. *India (Discovering Cultures).* Tarrytown, NY: Marshall Cavendish, 2003.
Nelson, Julie. *India (Ancient Civilizations).* Austin, TX: Raintree Steck-Vaughn, 2002.
Parker, Lewis K., and Linda Parker and D. King. *India (Dropping in On).* Vero Beach, FL: The Rourke
        Book Company, 2002.
Phillips, Douglas A., and Charles F. Gritzner and Thomas V. Peterson. *India (Modern World Nations).*
        Philadelphia, PA: Chelsea House Publishers, 2003.
Srinivasan, Radhika, and Leslie Jermyn. *India (Cultures of the World).* Tarrytown, NY: Marshall
        Cavendish, 2001.
Swan, Erin Pembrey. *India (Enchantment of the World).* New York: Children's Press, 2002.

Index

Page numbers in *italic* indicate illustrations.

Page numbers in *italic* indicate illustrations.